MW01000768

SHEPHERD'S NOTES

SHEPHERD'S NOTES

Bible Summary Series

The Old Testament

BROADMAN
&HOLMAN
PUBLISHERS

Nashville, Tennessee

Shepherd's Notes—*Old Testament*
© 2000
by Broadman & Holman Publishers
Nashville, Tennessee
All rights reserved
Printed in the United States of America

0–8054–9377–8

Dewey Decimal Classification: 221.6
Subject Heading: Bible. O.T.
Library of Congress Card Catalog Number: 99–053654

Library of Congress Cataloging-in-Publication Data

Gould, Dana, 1951
    Old Testament / by Dana Gould.
        p. cm.   — (Shepherd's notes.)
    Includes bibliographical references.
    ISBN 0–8054–9377–8
    1. Bible. O.T.—Study and teaching.   I. Title. II. Series.
    BS1193.G68 2000
    221.6'1—dc21   99–053654
                                                                                CIP

                    1 2 3 4 5 6   03 02 01 00
                              R

CONTENTS

FOREWORD

Dear Reader:

Shepherd's Notes are now available on every book in the Bible. In addition, we are pleased to provide a number of volumes in what we call **The Bible Summary Series**. This series will give you a perspective on various parts of the Bible that you wouldn't get by focusing on a book at a time. These volumes include *Old Testament, New Testament, Life & Teachings of Jesus, Life & Letters of Paul, Basic Christian Beliefs,* and *Manners & Customs of Bible Times.*

This particular volume, *Old Testament,* provides a quick and easy-to-read overview of the 39 books of the Old Testament. You can find a complete listing of all Shepherd's Notes on the back cover.

In Him,

David R. Shepherd
Editor-in-Chief

DESIGNED FOR THE BUSY USER

Shepherd's Notes for the Old Testament is designed to provide an easy-to-use tool for gaining information on the collection of Bible books the church calls the Old Testament. Other Shepherd's Notes volumes give a book-by-book presentation of Old Testament books. This volume steps back and takes a panoramic view of the Old Testament—the books that compose it, the types of literature represented, and the major themes found in these books.

Shepherd's Notes are for laymen, pastors, teachers, small-group leaders and participants, as well as the classroom student. Enrich your personal study or quiet time. Shorten your class or small-group preparation time as you gain valuable insights in the truths of God's Word that you can pass along to your students or group members.

DESIGNED FOR QUICK ACCESS

Those with time restraints will especially appreciate the timesaving features built in the *Shepherd's Notes*. All features are intended to aid a quick and concise encounter with the crux of the message.

Concise Information. The Old Testament is replete with characters, places, events, and instruction to believers. Short commentary sections provide quick "snapshots" of sections, highlighting important points and other information.

Brief Outlines. Comprehensive outlines cover each book of the Old Testament. This is a valuable feature for following the narrative's flow and allows for a quick, easy way to locate a particular passage.

Shepherd's Notes. These summary statements appear at the beginning of each book's treatment. They deliver the essence of the message presented in the sections that follow.

Icons. Various icons in the margin highlight key insights or themes, allowing the reader to search or trace those themes.

Sidebars and Charts. These specially selected features provide additional background information to aid your study or preparation. These include definitions as well as cultural, historical, and biblical insights.

Maps. These are placed at appropriate places in the book to aid your understanding and study of a text or passage.

In addition to the above features, for those readers who require or desire more information and resources for studying the Old Testament, a list of reference sources used for this volume suggests many works that allow the reader to extend the scope of his or her study of the Old Testament.

DESIGNED TO WORK FOR YOU

Personal Study. Using the *Shepherd's Notes* with a passage of Scripture can enlighten your study and take it to a new level. At your fingertips is information that would require searching several volumes to find. In addition, many points of application occur throughout the volume, contributing to personal growth.

Teaching Shepherd's Notes. Old Testament will be especially valuable for those teaching the Bible. It will enable them to see quickly the larger context of a book or a passage within that book. The outline format, summaries, and sidebars are designed for quick, easy access.

Group Study. Shepherd's Notes can be an excellent companion volume to use for gaining a quick but accurate understanding of the message of a Bible book. Each group member can benefit by having his or her own copy. The *Note's* format accommodates the study of each Old Testament book. Leaders may use its flexible features to prepare for group sessions or use it during group sessions.

LIST OF MARGIN ICONS USED IN OLD TESTAMENT OVERVIEW

Shepherd's Notes. Placed to indicate an Old Testament book summary. This is a capsule statement that provides the reader with the essence of the message of that particular book.

Old Testament Passage. An Old Testament passage that illuminates the passage being studied.

New Testament Passage. A New Testament passage that is either a fulfillment of prophecy or is foreshadowed by an Old Testament passage.

Quote. Used to identify an enlightening quote pertinent to the discussion of the text.

Word Picture. Indicates that the meaning of a specific word or phrase is illustrated so as to shed light on it.

Historical Context. To indicate background information—historical, biographical, cultural—and provide insight on understanding or interpreting a passage.

SECTION ONE: INTRODUCTION TO THE OLD TESTAMENT

The Old Testament is the first part of the sacred Scriptures Christians call the Bible. This set of writings is also sacred Scripture for Judaism. It tells of God's creation of the universe and His creation of Israel as a people through whom He will bless all peoples.

The first books of the Old Testament to become canonized were Genesis, Exodus, Leviticus, Numbers, and Deuteronomy, which collectively are known as the Torah. *Torah* means law, being derived from the Hebrew word for that term. These first five books are also called the Pentateuch, which is a word meaning "five fifths," the five-fifths of the law.

The second section to win approval was the prophetic section, which the Jews divided into Former Prophets and Latter Prophets. Their Former Prophets are what are now known as the historical books (Joshua, Judges, 1 and 2 Samuel, and 1 and 2 Kings). Their Latter Prophets include Isaiah, Jeremiah, Ezekiel, and the twelve minor prophets. This prophetic section was included in the canon after the Babylonian Exile.

The third section of the Old Testament to be considered as the authoritative Word of God, and therefore as part of the canon (about A.D. 90), was termed the Writings, and included Psalms, Proverbs, Job, Song of Solomon, Ruth, Lamentations, Ecclesiastes, Esther, Daniel, Ezra-Nehemiah, and 1 and 2 Chronicles. It is

The word *canon* comes from the Greek word for "reed." In the development of the usage of the word, canon came to mean a standard of measurement. Then canon developed to mean an official standard by which other things are measured.

readily seen that the Jews divided their Scriptures into these three main divisions: Law, Prophets, and Writings.

Jesus quoted from the Hebrew Scriptures time and again; He loved them, considered them as authoritative, and directed men to them as the spiritual guide for their lives (adapted from William W. Stevens, *A Guide for Old Testament Study*, [Nashville:Broadman & Holman, 1974], 19–21).

THE BOOKS OF THE OLD TESTAMENT

THE THIRTY-NINE OLD TESTAMENT BOOKS AND THEIR DIVISIONS

LAW	HISTORY	
Genesis	Joshua	2 Kings
Exodus	Judges	1 Chronicles
Leviticus	Ruth	2 Chronicles
Numbers	1 Samuel	Ezra
Deuteronomy	2 Samuel	Nehemiah
	1 Kings	Esther

MAJOR PROPHETS	MINOR PROPHETS	
Isaiah	Hosea	Nahum
Jeremiah	Joel	Habakkuk
Lamentations	Amos	Zephaniah
Ezekiel	Obadiah	Haggai
Daniel	Jonah	Zechariah
	Micah	Malachi

POETRY/WISDOM

Job	Ecclesiastes
Psalms	Song of Solomon
Proverbs	

THE PENTATEUCH

Pentateuch is one way of identifying these books. However, a more accurate and informative term is *Torah* (Hebrew *torah*). This name is based on the verb *yarah,* which means "to teach." *Torah* is, therefore, *teaching.* Careful attention to this will lead to an appreciation both of the contents of the Pentateuch and of its fundamental purpose: the instruction of God's people concerning Himself, themselves, and His purposes for them.

■ *The first five books of the Bible, the Pen-*
■ *tateuch, are commonly called the Five Books*
■ *of Moses. They make up one of three sections*
■ *of Hebrew Scripture referred to as the Law or*
■ *Torah. The other two sections are the Proph-*
■ *ets and the Writings. Jesus referred to Hebrew*
■ *Scripture's witness to Him as "the Law of*
■ *Moses, the Prophets and the Psalms"*
■ *(Luke 24:44).*

■ *Originally the Pentateuch was one book des-*
■ *ignated as the Book of Moses. By the time of*
■ *Christ, the book had been divided into five*
■ *books—Genesis, Exodus, Leviticus, Numbers,*
■ *and Deuteronomy. Various types of literature*
■ *make up the Pentateuch including narrative,*
■ *law, poetry, genealogies, and lists. These*
■ *diverse elements are woven together to give an*
■ *account of the creation of the universe to the*
■ *death of Moses.*

■ *The central focus of the Pentateuch is the exo-*
■ *dus of Israel from Egypt, God's covenant with*
■ *them at Sinai, their forty years wandering,*
■ *and finally preparation to possess the land*
■ *God promised. Genesis, which deals with*
■ *events preceding the exodus, sets the stage for*
■ *Exodus-Deuteronomy and provides for the*
■ *generation about to enter the Promised Land,*
■ *both historical and theological understanding*

- *of where they have come from and who God*
- *has called them to be. Their constant aware-*
- *ness of who they are and their imparting that*
- *knowledge to the generations to come is a key*
- *purpose for The Book of Moses.*

GENESIS

- *Genesis in a Nutshell: Genesis is the first*
- *book of the Bible. It opens with God's cre-*
- *ation of the universe including human*
- *beings. Here we see the origin of sin and*
- *God's first steps in providing a remedy.*

Genesis 1–11. This first section provides the universal setting for Israel's story. Genesis opens with God's creating the universe. The focus narrows to creation of the first family (1:1–2:25). Trust in a wily serpent rather than in God brings sin into the world and shows God's judgment on sin as well as His merciful grace to sinners.

Sin multiplies to the extent that God has to send a flood (see p. 6) through which God eliminates all humanity except the family of Noah. God then makes a covenant with that family never again to bring such punishment (6:1–9:17), but human sin continues on the individual and the societal levels, bringing necessary divine punishment of the nations at the tower of Babel (9:18–11:9).

The book of Genesis takes its name from the Greek version of the Old Testament (the Septuagint), which called it *Genesis,* meaning "beginning."

Genesis 12–36. This section details the Patriarchal Period. God establishes a plan to redeem and bless the humanity that persists in sin. He calls one man of faith—Abraham—and leads him to a new beginning in a new land. He gives His promises of land, nation, fame, and a mission of blessing for the nations. This works itself

THE FLOOD

The cataclysmic deluge described in Genesis 6–9:17 as God's judgment on the earth is mentioned elsewhere in the Old Testament (Gen. 10:1,32; 11:10; Pss. 29:10; 104:6-9; Isa. 54:9) and in the New Testament (Matt. 24:38-39; Luke 17:26-27; Heb. 11:7; 1 Pet. 3:20; 2 Pet. 2:5; 3:3-7). That more verses are devoted to the flood than to the creation (Gen. 1–2) or the fall (Gen. 3) suggests the significance of the account.

The Old Testament Account

Because of the great wickedness of humanity (Gen. 6:5,11), God resolved to destroy all living beings (6:13) with the exception of righteous Noah and his family (6:9,18). God instructed Noah to make an ark of cypress wood (6:14; "gopher wood," KJV). He told Noah to take his family and seven [pairs] of every clean species and two of every unclean species of animals, birds, and creeping things, along with provisions for the duration of the flood (6:18-21; 7:1-3). The rains lasted forty days and nights, covered "all the high mountains under the entire heavens" (7:19), and destroyed every living crea-

ture on land (7:21-23). When Noah and his family emerged from the ark after a year and ten days, he built an altar and offered sacrifices to God (8:14-20). God blessed Noah and his family (9:1) and made a covenant that He would never again destroy the earth by flood (8:21; 9:11). God gave the rainbow as a visible sign of that covenant (9:12-17).

Date and Extent of the Flood

It is impossible to determine the exact date of the flood, since no archaeological or geological materials have been found that would enable its accurate dating. Estimates have placed it between 13,000 and 3000 B.C.

The extent of the flood has been debated. Arguments for a universal flood include: (1) the wording of Genesis 6–9, which is best interpreted as a universal flood (see 7:19-23); (2) the widespread flood traditions among many, widely scattered peoples that are best explained if all peoples are descended from Noah; (3) the unusual source of water (Gen. 7:11); (4) the length of the flood, whereas a local flood would have subsided in a few days; (5) the false assumption that all life resided in a limited geographical area; and (6) God's limitless ability to

act within history.

Arguments against a universal flood have persuaded some scholars to accept a limited flood. Some arguments are: (1) the amount of water needed to cover the highest mountain, which would be eight times as much as there is on earth; (2) the practical problems of housing and feeding so many animals for a year; (3) the destruction of all plant life submerged in salt water for over a year; (4) the view that destruction of the human race required only a flood covering the part of the earth inhabited at that time; and (5) the lack of geological evidence for a worldwide cataclysm. While all of our questions cannot be answered, the biblical data points in the direction of a universal flood.

Theological Significance

(1) The flood demonstrates God's hatred of sin and the certainty of His judgment on it. (2) God's giving people 120 years to repent before judgment came demonstrates His patience in dealing with sin. (3) The sparing of one family demonstrates God's saving grace. (4) The flood reveals God's rule over nature and over humanity.

out in blessing nations that help Abraham and punishing those who do not. It climaxes in God's covenant with Abraham in which Abraham shows faithfulness in the sign of circumcision (see p. 8).

New generations led by Isaac and Jacob find God continuing to lead them, to call them to be His people, and to renew His promises to them. Human trickery and deception personified in Jacob do not alter God's determination to carry out His redemptive plan.

Genesis 37–50. This last section is the story of Joseph. It is the finest example of historical narrative in the book of Genesis. The hero is Joseph, the ideal man, whom God used to deliver His people.

EXODUS

■ *Exodus in a Nutshell: If Genesis is the book*
■ *of beginnings, Exodus is the book of redemp-*
■ *tion.*

Exodus 1–11. When Exodus opens, Israel is enslaved in Egypt. The God of Abraham, Isaac, and Jacob calls Moses to deliver Israel from slavery and lead them to the land God promised Abraham. As would be expected, Pharaoh resists. God then initiates a cycle of nine plagues to persuade Pharaoh to liberate His people.

Exodus 12–14. Pharaoh repents until the plagues cease and then reverts to his resistance against God. God sends the tenth plague—the death of the oldest son in each Egyptian family. God's people are redeemed by the blood of the Passover lamb (12:1–28). Pharaoh urges Israel to

Exodus, meaning "way out," was the title the early Greek translation, the Septuagint, gave to the second book of the Torah (compare Exod. 19:1).

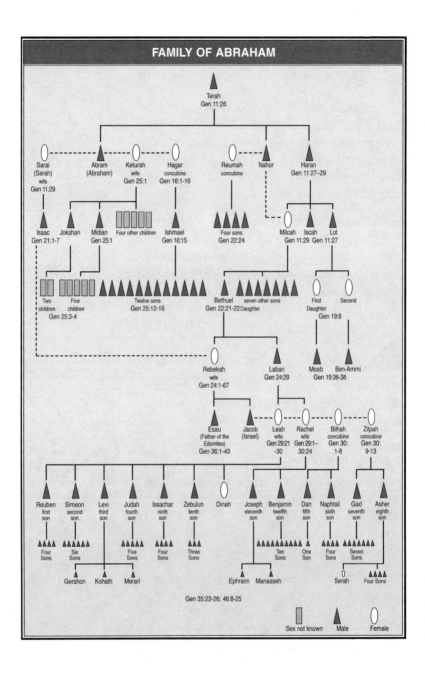

FAMILY OF ABRAHAM

Terah
Gen 11:26

Sarai (Sarah) wife Gen 11:29

Abram (Abraham)

Keturah wife Gen 25:1

Hagar concubine Gen 16:1-16

Reumah concubine

Nahor

Haran Gen 11:27–29

Isaac Gen 21:1-7

Jokshan

Midian Gen 25:1

Four other children

Ishmael Gen 16:15

Four sons Gen 22:24

Milcah Gen 11:29

Iscah Gen 11:27

Lot

Two children

Five children Gen 25:3-4

Twelve sons Gen 25:12-16

Bethuel Gen 22:21-22 Daughter

seven other sons

First Daughter

Second Gen 19:8

Rebekah wife Gen 24:1-67

Laban Gen 24:29

Moab Gen 19:36-38

Ben-Ammi

Esau (Father of the Edomites) Gen 36:1-43

Jacob (Israel)

Leah wife Gen 29:21 -30

Rachel wife Gen 29:1– 30:24

Bilhah concubine Gen 30: 1-8

Zilpah concubine Gen 30: 9-13

Reuben first son

Simeon second son

Levi third son

Judah fourth son

Issachar ninth son

Zebulun tenth son

Dinah

Joseph eleventh son

Benjamin twelfth son

Dan fifth son

Naphtali sixth son

Gad seventh son

Asher eighth son

Four Sons

Six Sons

Five Sons

Four Sons

Three Sons

Gershon   Kohath   Merari

Ten Sons

One Son

Four Sons

Seven Sons

Ephraim   Manasseh

Serah

Four Sons

Gen 35:23-26; 46:8-25

Sex not known   Male   Female

leave but then decides to pursue them. God delivers His people through the Red Sea and destroys the pursuing Egyptians (see p. 11).

Exodus 15–18. God's people enter into training for their holy calling. As God's people, not only do they need to be delivered from their bondage, but they also need to be educated in the ways of righteousness and instructed in godliness.

Exodus 19–34. At Mount Sinai the Israelites are shown that they are a people set apart for God to do a peculiar work. Since they are to be the recipients of divine revelation for the benefit of all mankind, the laws and regulations about to be given to them differ from those of all other nations. Israel is to be a kingdom of priests and a holy nation (see p. 10).

Exodus 35–40. The book of Exodus moves us to a climax in the setting up of the tabernacle and the establishment of the official worship of the redeemed nation. When the tabernacle is complete, God's presence fills it.

THE TEN PLAGUES OF EGYPT	
PLAGUE	**SCRIPTURE**
1. WATER TO BLOOD—The waters of the Nile turned to blood.	Exod 7:14-25
2. FROGS—Frogs infested the land of Egypt.	Exod 8:1-15
3. GNATS (Mosquitoes)—Small stinging insects infested the land of Egypt.	Exod 8:16-19
4. FLIES—Swarms of flies, possibly a biting variety, infested the land of Egypt.	Exod 8:20-32
5. PLAGUE ON THE CATTLE—A serious disease, possibly anthrax, infested the cattle belonging to the Egyptians.	Exod 9:1-7
6. BOILS—A skin disease infected the Egyptians.	Exod 9:8-12
7. HAIL—A storm that destroyed the grain fields of Egypt but spared the land of Goshen inhabited by the Israelites.	Exod 9:13-35
8. LOCUSTS—An infestation of locusts stripped the land of Egypt of plant life.	Exod 10:1-20
9. DARKNESS—A deep darkness covered the land of Egypt for three days.	Exod 10:21-29
10. DEATH OF THE FIRSTBORN—The firstborn of every Egyptian family died.	Exod 11:1–12:30

THE TEN COMMANDMENTS

COMMANDMENT	PASSAGE	RELATED OLD TESTAMENT PASSAGES	RELATED NEW TESTAMENT PASSAGES	JESUS' TEACHINGS
You shall have no other gods before me	Exod 20:3; Deut 5:7	Exod 34:14; Deut 6:4,13-14; 2 Kgs 17:35; Ps 81:9; Jer 25:6; 35:15	Acts 5:29	Matt 4:10; 6:33; 22:37-40
You shall not make for yourself an idol	Exod 20:4-6; Deut 5:8-10	Exod 20:23; 32:8; 34:17; Lev 19:4; 26:1; Deut 4:15-20; 7:25; 32:21; Ps 115:4-7; Isa 44:12-20	Acts 17:29; 1 Cor 8:4-6,10-14; 1 John 5:21	Matt 6:24; Luke 16:13
You shall not misuse the name of the Lord	Exod 20:7; Deut 5:11	Exod 22:28; Lev 18:21; 19:12; 22:2; 24:16; Ezek 39:7	Rom 2:23-24; Jas 5:12	Matt 5:33-37; 6:9; 23:16-22
Remember the Sabbath day by keeping it holy	Exod 20:8-11; Deut 5:12-15	Gen 2:3; Exod 16:23-30; 31:13-16; 35:2-3; Lev 19:30; Isa 56:2; Jer 17:21-27	Acts 20:7; Heb 10:25	Matt 12:1-13; Mark 2:23-27; 3:1-6; Luke 6:1-11
Honor your father and your mother	Exod 20:12; Deut 5:16	Exod 21:17; Lev 19:3; Deut 21:18-21; 27:16; Prov 6:20	Eph 6:1-3; Col 3:20	Matt 15:4-6; 19:19; Mark 7:9-13; Luke 18:20
You shall not murder	Exod 20:13; Deut 5:17	Gen 9:6; Lev 24:17; Num 35:33	Rom 13:9-10; I Pet 4:15	Matt 5:21-24; 19:18; Mark 10:19; Luke 18:20
You shall not commit adultery	Exod 20:14; Deut 5:18	Lev 18:20; 20:10; Deut 22:22; Num 5:12-31; Prov 6:29,32	Rom 13:9-10; 1 Cor 6:9; Heb 13:4; Jas 2:11	Matt 5:27-30; 19:18; Mark 10:19; Luke 18:20
You shall not steal	Exod 20:15; Deut 5:19	Lev 19:11,13; Ezek 18:7	Rom 13:9-10; Eph 4:28; Jas 5:4	Matt 19:18; Mark 10:19; Luke 18:20
You shall not give false testimony	Exod 20:16; Deut 5:20	Exod 23:1, 7; Lev 19:11; Pss 15:2; 101:5; Prov 10:18; Jer 9:3-5; Zech 8:16	Eph 4:25,31; Col 3:9; Titus 3:2	Matt 5:37; 19:18; Mark 10:19; Luke 18:20
You shall not covet	Exod 20:17; Deut 5:21	Deut 7:25; Job 31:24-28; Ps 62:10	Rom 7:7; 13:9; Eph 5:3-5; Heb 13:5; Jas 4:1-2	Luke 12:15-34

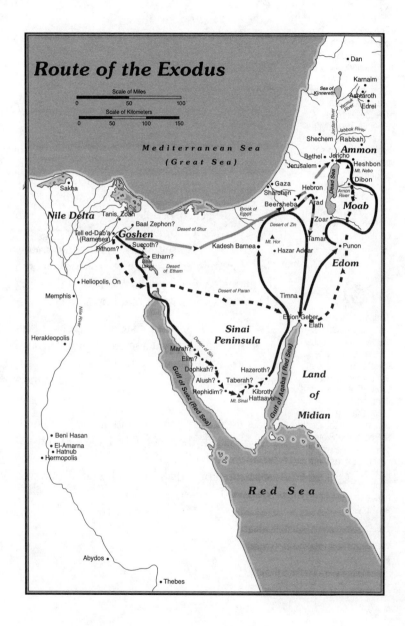

Route of the Exodus

Scale of Miles
0   50   100

Scale of Kilometers
0   50   100   150

Mediterranean Sea
(Great Sea)

Dan

Karnaim

Sea of
Kinnereth

Ashtaroth

Edrei

Jordan River

Yarmuk
River

Jabbok River

Shechem   Rabbah

Ammon

Bethel   Jericho

Jerusalem

Heshbon

Mt. Nebo

Dibon

Sakha

Nile Delta

Tanis, Zoan

Baal Zephon?

Tell ed-Dab'a
(Rameses)

Goshen

Pithom?

Succoth?

Etham?

Bitter
Lakes

Desert
of Etham

Gaza

Sharuhen

Beersheba

Hebron

Arad

Moab

Brook of
Egypt

Desert of Shur

Desert of Zin

Zoar

Tamar

Amon
River

Dead Sea

Kadesh Barnea

Mt. Hor

Hazar Addar

Punon

Edom

Heliopolis, On

Desert of Paran

Memphis

Nile River

Timna

Ezion Geber

Elath

Herakleopolis

Sinai
Peninsula

Mareh?

Desert of Sin

Elim?

Gulf of Suez (Red Sea)

Dophkah?

Alush?

Rephidim?

Taberah?

Hazeroth?

Kibroth
Hattaavah?

Gulf of Aqaba (Red Sea)

Land

of

Midian

Mt. Sinai

Beni Hasan

El-Amarna

Hatnub

Hermopolis

Red Sea

Abydos

Thebes

11

LEVITICUS

The name *Leviticus* comes from the ancient Greek translation, the Septuagint, which titled the composition *Leueitikon*, that is, *The Book of the Levites*. The Levites are not, however, the major characters of this book. The title rather points to the book as useful to the Levites in their ministry as worship leaders and teachers of morals.

Today Leviticus is the least appreciated of the five books of the Pentateuch. Many believe that it doesn't apply to Christians today. But Leviticus is important today in being the first detailed revelation of the living theme of the Bible as a whole—the way by which God restores lost people to Himself. "You must be holy because I, the LORD, am holy. I have set you apart from all other people to be my very own" (Lev. 20:26, NLT).

■ *Leviticus in a Nutshell: Leviticus communi-*
■ *cates the awesome holiness of God and*
■ *instructs Israel in how to approach Him.*

Leviticus cannot be understood apart from God's desire to be with His covenant people, Israel. But because a Holy God cannot condone sin, Israel's experiment in idolatry with the golden calf (Exod. 32) presented God with a dilemma. Twice God warned the Israelites: "You are a stiff-necked people. If I were to go with you even for a moment, I might destroy you" (Exod. 33:5; also see 33:3). How could a holy God continue to go with a disobedient and rebellious people? Exodus 34–40 and the book of Leviticus answer that question.

Leviticus 1–16. The first sixteen chapters of Leviticus therefore present a series of typical actions that picture the way God redeems the lost, separating them from their sin and its consequences.

Leviticus 17–27. This second half of Leviticus centers on the theme of holy living and consists of a prescribed "holiness code" (17:1–26:46) and an appendix on voluntary devotion (27:1–34).

NUMBERS

- *Numbers in a Nutshell: Israel travels to the*
- *edge of Canaan but refuses to fight for the*
- *Promised Land. Because they reject God's*
- *promise, He sentences them to forty years in*
- *the desert.*

Moses had led the Israelites from Mount Sinai to the borders of the Promised Land. The concluding verse suggests that Numbers instructs Israel in the preconditions of their possession and enjoyment of the Promised Land.

Background. The Hebrew name of this book (*bemidbar*) means "in the desert" and is thus a most appropriate way of describing its contents as a treatise whose entire setting is in the Sinai, Negev, and Trans-jordanian wilderness. The English title "Numbers" translates *Arithmoi*, the title used by the ancient Greek translation, the Septuagint.

SACRIFICIAL SYSTEM			
NAME	REFERENCE	ELEMENTS	SIGNIFICANCE
Burnt Offering	Lev 1; 6:8-13	Bull, ram, male goat, male dove, or young pigeon without blemish. (Always male animals, but species of animal varied according to individual's economic status.)	Voluntary. Signifies propitiation for sin and complete surrender, devotion, and commitment to God.
Grain Offering Also called Meal, or Tribute, Offering	Lev 2; 6:14-23	Flour, bread, or grain made with olive oil and salt (always unleavened); or incense.	Voluntary. Signifies thanksgiving for firstfruits.
Fellowship Offering Also called Peace Offering: includes (1) Thank Offering, (2) Vow Offering, and (3) Freewill Offering	Lev 3; 7:11-36	Any animal without blemish. (Species of animal varied according to individual's economic status.)	Voluntary. Symbolizes fellowship with God. (1) Signifies thankfulness for a specific blessing; (2) offers a ritual expression of a vow; and (3) symbolizes general thankfulness (to be brought to one of three required religious services).
Sin Offering	Lev 4:1–5:13; 6:24-30; 12:6-8	Male or female animal without blemish—as follows: bull for high priest and congregation; male goat for king; female goat or lamb for common person; dove or pigeon for slightly poor; tenth of an ephah of flour for the very poor.	Mandatory. Made by one who had sinned unintentionally or was unclean in order to attain purification.
Guilt Offering	Lev 5:14–6:7; 7:1-6; 14:12-18	Ram or lamb without blemish.	Mandatory. Made by a person who had either deprived another of his rights or had desecrated something holy.

JEWISH FEASTS AND FESTIVALS

NAME	MONTH: DATE	REFERENCE	SIGNIFICANCE
Passover	Nisan (Mar./Apr.): 14-21	Exod 12:2-20; Lev 23:5	Commemorates God's deliverence of Israel out of Egypt.
Feast of Unleavened Bread	Nisan (Mar./Apr.): 15-21	Lev 23:6-8	Commemorates God's deliverence of Israel out of Egypt. Includes a Day of Firstfruits for the barley harvest.
Feast of Weeks, or Harvest (Pentecost)	Sivan (May/June): 6 (seven weeks after Passover)	Exod 23:16; 34:22; Lev 23:15-21	Commemorates the giving of the law at Mount Sinai. Includes a Day of Firstfruits for the wheat harvest.
Feast of Trumpets (Rosh Hashanah)	Tishri (Sept./Oct.): 1	Lev 23:23-25 Num 29:1-6	Day of the blowing of the trumpets to signal the beginning of the civil new year.
Day of Atonement (Yom Kippur)	Tishri (Sept./Oct.): 10	Lev 23:26-33; Exod 30:10	On this day the high priest makes atonement for the nation's sin. Also a day of fasting.
Feast of Booths, or Tabernacles (Sukkot)	Tishri (Sept./Oct.): 15-21	Lev 23:33-43; Num 29:12-39; Deut 16:13	Commemorates the forty years of wilderness wandering.
Feast of Dedication, or Festival of Lights (Hanukkah)	Kislev (Nov./Dec.): 25-30; and Tebeth (Dec./Jan.): 1-2	John 10:22	Commemorates the purification of the temple by Judas Maccabaeus in 164 B.C.
Feast of Purim, or Esther	Adar (Feb./Mar.): 14	Esth 9	Commemorates the deliverance of the Jewish people in the days of Esther.

Numbers 1:1–10:10. The covenant with Israel has been concluded at Sinai. Its social, political, and religious stipulations have been outlined (Exod. 20–40). Then the Lord commands His people to leave the holy mountain and to make their way to the Promised Land.

Numbers 10:11–14:45. A little more than a year after the Exodus and nearly a year at Sinai, Israel presses on to the land of promise, mobilized for conquest. Taking their cue from the movement of the cloud of glory, the camp sets out in the manner previously commanded. Preceding the whole camp is the ark of God, the symbol of His guiding and protecting presence.

The last verse of Numbers summarizes the whole by saying, "These are the commands and regulations the LORD gave through Moses to the Israelites on the plains of Moab by the Jordan across from Jericho" (Num. 36:13).

Numbers 15:1–22:1. With striking irony, the Lord, who has just sentenced the people of Israel to death in the wilderness, outlines immediately the principles of sacrifice and service to be followed by their descendants in the land of Canaan.

Numbers 22:1–25:18. The defeat of the Amorites and Bashanites suggests the way is clear for Israel's conquest of the Promised Land. Before entering the land, Israel would, however, face obstacles to God's promise of land. The first obstacle was external—the threat of curse from Balaam; the second, internal—the threat of compromise to the sexual standards of the Moabites.

History depends on God's leadership and human obedience, not on military statistics or human expectations. At the same time, God works through humans and human organizations to accomplish His purposes.

Numbers 26:1–36:13. Having now cleared the way for the crossing of the Jordan and the conquest of Canaan, the Lord gives instructions concerning those matters. He first orders a new census of the tribes and outlines some principles of land inheritance in families where there are no sons. The earnest desire of the daughters of Zelophehad to share in God's gift of land contrasts sharply with the earlier generation's spurning of the gift.

"The LORD heard your request and said to me, 'I have heard what the people have said to you, and they are right. Oh, that they would always have hearts like this, that they might fear me and obey all my commands! If they did, they and their descendants would prosper forever'" (Deut. 5:28–29, NLT).

DEUTERONOMY

- ■ *Deuteronomy in a Nutshell: Israel had come*
- ■ *to the edge of the Promised Land but refused*
- ■ *to fight for it. Because they rejected God's*
- ■ *promise, He sentences them to forty years in*
- ■ *the desert. With some exceptions, the genera-*
- ■ *tion that rebelled against God had died. Now*
- ■ *thirty-eight years later, Moses is preparing*
- ■ *Israel to possess the land promised to them.*

Deuteronomy is structured as three main discourses (or sermons) with three short appendixes (or sermons).

Discourse One. The first discourse (1:1–4:43) is mainly historical and hortatory. Moses rehearses in broad outline the experiences from Horeb to Moab and exhorts the Israelites to cleave to Yahweh and steer clear of idolatry.

Discourse Two. The second discourse (4:44–26:19) is principally hortatory and legislative. This is the longest discourse and constitutes the nucleus of the book. It gives a summary of the civil, moral, and religious laws and statutes of Israel. The tone is that of a father speaking. The ideal is holiness.

Discourse Three. The third discourse (27:1–31:30) is predictive and threatening. It deals primarily with the blessings of obedience and the curses of disobedience.

Following these three discourses are three appendixes:

Moses' song (chap. 32)
Moses' blessing (chap. 33)
The account of Moses' death and burial (chap. 34).

- *The Historical Books in the English Bible are*
- *Joshua, Judges, Ruth, 1 and 2 Samuel, 1 and*
- *2 Kings, 1 and 2 Chronicles, Ezra,*
- *Nehemiah, and Esther. At first, the books of*
- *1 and 2 Samuel were one book, as were*
- *Kings, Chronicles, and Ezra–Nehemiah. The*
- *Septuagint, the ancient Greek translation,*
- *was the first to divide the books. The Latin*
- *Vulgate and English versions have continued*
- *this practice. (The Hebrew division of these*
- *books did not occur until the Middle Ages.)*
- *Our English translators, again following the*
- *Septuagint, arranged the Historical Books in*
- *a loosely chronological order.*

The Former Prophets (Joshua, Judges, Samuel, and Kings) continue the narrative of Genesis through Deuteronomy, which tells of Israel's birth and rise as a nation. Deuteronomy concludes with the appointment of Joshua as Moses' successor who eventually leads Israel into the land. Joshua through 2 Kings relates the occupation of the land of Canaan and the rise of the Hebrew monarchy and concludes with the destruction and exile of the nation by the Babylonian Empire.

Ruth and Esther are included among the five *Megilloth*. These books—Song of Solomon, Ruth, Lamentations, Ecclesiastes, and Esther—are related to the five festivals (and fasts) of the Jewish calendar.

JOSHUA

■ *Joshua in a Nutshell: Under Joshua's lead-*
■ *ership, the people of God enter the land of*
■ *rest promised to their ancestors. Here*
■ *Joshua leads Israel's conquest of Canaan.*
■ *Israel divides the land and chooses to live as*
■ *a covenant community within their inher-*
■ *ited land.*

Under Joshua's leadership, the people of God entered into the land of rest promised to their ancestors, because the people were careful not to depart from the "Book of the Law" of Moses (1:8).

Joshua 1:1–5:15. The opening section shows how God enables Israel to enter the land. The commander is chosen and the land surveyed. The people cross the Jordan with the help of the Lord, and a memorial is established for future generations. Once in the land, the people renew their commitment to the Lord and worship in celebration.

Joshua 6:1–12:24. Joshua directs three campaigns in Canaan. The central campaign includes Jericho, Ai, and Gibeon. The southern campaign is against a five-king coalition led by the king of Jerusalem. The northern campaign is against a coalition of city-states led by Hazor. Through these battles the people learn that Yahweh fights for them and secures their victory.

Joshua 13:1–21:45. The detailed description of Israel's inheritance may be tedious to modern readers. For the author it proves the faithfulness of God's Word. The territories given by Moses

The Conquest of Canaan

Central Campaign
Southern Campaign
Northern Campaign

Today there still is a battle between those who are God's people and those who are not. The victorious outcome of this battle is assured for God's people. Joshua is filled with the assurance that God is victorious over those who oppose Him.

are listed first and then the land distributed by Joshua.

Joshua 22:1–24:28. This section shows how Israel preserves itself in the land by carefully observing the word of the Lord. Joshua exhorts them to live in faith, and the people enter into a covenant to serve the Lord. This serves as an example of how future generations are to live in commitment to one another and to God.

JUDGES

■ *Judges in a Nutshell: Chaos reigns because*
■ *Israel disobeys the covenant and the people*
■ *have no king. Although the people inherit the*
■ *land of promise, they repeatedly disregard*
■ *their covenant obligations (21:25). Israel's*
■ *disobedience results in their oppression at*
■ *the hands of neighboring peoples (3:7–8).*
■ *Such oppression leads Israel to cry to the*
■ *Lord for help (3:9). God responds to Israel's*
■ *repentance and its cries for mercy by sending*
■ *judges or deliverers (3:9–10). Israel, how-*
■ *ever, returns to disobedience following the*
■ *death of the judge (3:11–12).*

The book of Judges continues the unfolding story of Israel's life in the land promised to their fathers.

The judges were not trained arbiters of legal cases as the word *judge* means today. They were Spirit-endowed leaders who were chosen by God for specific tasks (compare 3:9–10; 6:34; 11:29; 13:25). As judges, they worked to bring about justice for the oppressed people of Israel. To avoid confusion with the modern connotation of *judged*, the NIV has translated "lead/led"

JUDGES OF THE OLD TESTAMENT

NAME	REFERENCE	IDENTIFICATION
Othniel	Judg 1:12-13; 3:7-11	Conquered a Canaanite city
Ehud	Judg 3:12-30	Killed Eglon, king of Moab, and defeated Moabites
Shamgar	Judg 3:31	Killed 600 Philistines with an oxgoad
Deborah	Judg 4–5	Convinced Barak to lead an army to victory against Sisera's troops
Gideon	Judg 6–8	Led 300 men to victory against 135,000 Midianites
Tola	Judg 10:1-2	Judged for 23 years
Jair	Judg 10:3-5	Judged for 22 years
Jephthah	Judg 11:1–12:7	Defeated the Ammonites after making a promise to the Lord
Ibzan	Judg 12:8-10	Judged for 7 years
Elon	Judg 12:11-12	Judged for 10 years
Abdon	Judg 12:13-15	Judged for 8 years
Samson	Judg 13–16	Killed 1,000 Philistines with a donkey's jawbone; was deceived by Delilah; destroyed a Philistine temple; judged 20 years
Samuel	1 and 2 Sam	Was the last of the judges and the first of the prophets

"In those days Israel had no king, so the people did whatever seemed right in their own eyes" (Judg. 21:25, NLT).

Background. The book of Ruth is named for its heroine, whose devotion to God and love for family have endeared her to generations of readers. It tells us how God graciously rewarded the faithfulness of the widows Ruth and Naomi by delivering them through heir kinsman-redeemer Boaz, who married Ruth and maintained the property of Naomi's family. The story takes place during the time of the Judges (about 1150 B.C.). For this reason our English versions and the Greek translation of the Old Testament put the book after the book of Judges.

in many passages where it is more appropriate in context (4:4; 10:2–3; 12:8–11, 13–14; 15:20; 16:31). The verb *led* is used most often by the author to describe the judges' function. The judges also "saved" and "delivered" Israel from their enemies (e.g., 3:9, 31; 4:14; 10:1; 13:5).

Judges 1:1–3:6. This introductory section explains that Israel fails in the land because of its disobedience, immorality, and intermarriage with the Canaanites.

Judges 3:7–16:31. This section describes the seven cycles of Israel's sin and salvation by telling the stories of Israel's judges. These judges include Othniel, Ehud and Shamgar, Deborah and Barak, Gideon, Tola and Jair, Jephthah and Ibzan, Elon, Addon, and Samson.

Judges 17:1–21:25. The final section of the book gives two examples of Israel's moral defection. The first case concerns idolatry by the tribe of Dan (Judg. 17–18). The second case involves intertribal warfare that results from the rape and murder of a Levite's concubine by the men of Benjamin (Judg. 19–21).

RUTH

■ *Ruth in a Nutshell: Ruth is a story of faithful-*
■ *ness, both human and divine. Each of the*
■ *human characters demonstrates faithfulness*
■ *in the midst of difficult circumstances.*

Ruth 1. Ruth, a widow, faces a dilemma. Because of famine the family of Elimelech moved from Bethlehem to Moab. Elimelech died and left Naomi and her sons behind. The sons married Moabite women, Ruth and Orpah. Then the sons died, leaving the Moabite widows and Naomi without the security of a husband or sons. Naomi decides to return to Bethlehem. She urges Orpah and Ruth to stay in Moab and remarry. Ruth insists on returning with Naomi.

Ruth 2. Ruth meets Boaz, who invites her to work exclusively in his fields. He rewards Ruth with roasted grain and instructs laborers to leave stalks behind for her to glean. Naomi exults in the Lord when she learns about Boaz because she knows that he is a kinsman-redeemer.

Ruth 3. Naomi instructs Ruth to prepare herself properly and approach Boaz during the night at the threshing floor. She obeys. Ruth secretly approaches Boaz, trusting God to use Boaz to answer her needs and protect her.

Ruth 4. Boaz informs an unnamed kinsman that Naomi's fields are his to redeem (4:1–4). The kinsman agrees to buy the fields, but Boaz adds that whoever buys the land ought to marry Ruth to "maintain the name of the dead with his property" (v. 5). The Mosaic law did not tie the role of purchasing property with the custom of kinsman marriage. Therefore the kinsman could have declined without embarrassment. The kinsman explains that marriage would jeopardize his own inheritance. Boaz happily announces that he will redeem the property and marry Ruth himself.

God rewards the couple by giving them the child Obed, King David's grandfather. The women of the city praise God and recognize that Obed will sustain Naomi and possess Elimelech's property. In this sense Naomi is regarded the mother of the child (4:17).

Because of the faithfulness of Ruth and the faithfulness of God, the promises of the patriarchs could be realized through David and his greater Son, Jesus Christ: "A record of the genealogy of Jesus Christ, the son of David, the son of Abraham" (Matt 1:1).

God worked through a woman outside Israel to bring about His purposes for Israel and for all nations. Human categories and boundaries do not limit God as He works out His purpose.

1 SAMUEL

- *First Samuel in a Nutshell: Through the pro-*
- *phetic ministry of Samuel, God establishes*
- *the monarchy of Israel by choosing David, "a*
- *man after his own heart," to rule over His*
- *people (13:14). The book helps us see that*
- *God is Lord over history. His sovereign plans*
- *are accomplished in spite of human failure.*

1 Samuel 1–7. In the opening section the godly life of Samuel is distinguished from the failures of the high priest Eli and his sons, Hophni and Phinehas (1 Sam. 1–3). Although Samuel and the sons of Eli are reared in the same house, their dedication and destinies are very different. The Philistine wars lead to the end of Eli's family (1 Sam. 4), but Samuel prevails over the Philistines and leads Israel as judge and prophet (1 Sam. 7).

1 Samuel 8–15. Israel's disappointment with the priesthood of Eli and the sin of Eli's sons lead Israel to turn to a new form of leadership. The people, following the example of the nations around them, demand a king (1 Sam. 8). God grants their desires, and Samuel reluctantly appoints a king (1 Sam. 9–10). Saul's reign has a promising beginning (1 Sam. 11). King Saul, however, proves unlike Samuel because he does not listen to the word of the Lord (1 Sam. 13–15). The Lord thus rejects Saul as he had the house of Eli.

1 Samuel 16–31. The book's final section focuses on the personalities of Saul and David. Although Saul is king until the end of the book, the story turns to his successor's rise (1 Sam.

Background. First and 2 Samuel are named for the principle character in the early chapters of the book. Samuel led Israel as its last judge and anointed Israel's first two kings, Saul and David.

First and 2 Samuel were originally one book in the Hebrew Bible. The Greek Septuagint and the Latin Vulgate first divided the Hebrew into two books.

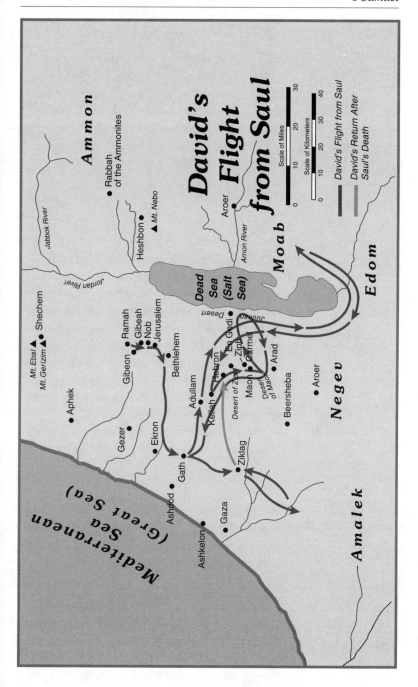

David's Flight from Saul

Scale of Miles
0 10 20 30

Scale of Kilometers
0 10 20 30 40

David's Flight from Saul
David's Return After
Saul's Death

Mediterranean Sea (Great Sea)

Ammon
Rabbah of the Ammonites
Jabbok River
Heshbon
Mt. Nebo
Jordan River
Dead Sea (Salt Sea)
Aroer
Arnon River
Moab
Edom
Mt. Ebal
Mt. Gerizim
Shechem
Aphek
Gezer
Gibeon
Ramah
Gibeah
Nob
Jerusalem
Ekron
Bethlehem
Adullam
Keilah
Hebron
Desert of Ziph
En Gedi
Ziph
Carmel
Maon
Desert of Maon
Arad
Judean Desert
Gath
Ashdod
Ziklag
Beersheba
Aroer
Negev
Gaza
Ashkelon
Amalek

16–17). David's story is told from the viewpoint of Saul's continued failures. Saul's reign was chaotic, marred by personal problems and the threat of Philistine oppression. While it became clearer that Saul was unfit for leadership, David emerged before the nation as God's champion to defeat the Philistines and rule the land (1 Sam.18–30). In the end, Saul takes his own life (1 Sam. 31).

2 SAMUEL

- *Second Samuel in a Nutshell: God consoli-*
- *dates the kingdom through the reign of*
- *David, who unifies the nation, conquers*
- *Israel's foes, and receives God's covenantal*
- *promise of an eternal dynasty and kingdom*
- *(7:5–16). Though David has sinned, God's*
- *grace proves greater than David's sin.*
- *Though David suffers consequences of his*
- *sin, God continues to watch over him and*
- *preserve his rule. Through David, God*
- *blesses Israel with its next king (Solomon)*
- *and, in time, with Jesus, its Messiah.*

There is no clearer demonstration in the Old Testament that we are valued by God "while we were still sinners" (Rom. 5:8) than the account of David. It is a testimony to God's grace that David overcame his sin to become the model for all kings to come.

2 Samuel 1–10. This section of the book traces the triumphs of David's reign, first over the tribe of Judah (chaps. 1–4) and then over all Israel (chaps. 5–6). The high point of David's career is the covenant the Lord makes with David and his descendants (chap. 7). Because of God's blessing, David successfully expands his kingdom by defeating Israel's enemies (chaps. 8–10).

2 Samuel 11–20. The sin of David and Bathsheba (chaps. 11–12) changes the tenor of the story from David's triumphs to his troubles. The following events (chaps. 13–20) tell the consequences of their sin as David's kingdom was rocked by moral and political problems.

2 Samuel 21–24. The last section of the book is an appendix to David's career as the Lord's anointed. Here the emphasis falls on David's praise for God's sovereign mercies (chap. 22) and the mighty warriors the Lord uses in the service of the king (chap. 23). The stories of famine, war, and pestilence resulting from Israel's sin are fitting reminders that no king is above the word of the Lord (chaps. 21; 24).

1 KINGS

■ *First Kings in a Nutshell: God establishes*
■ *Solomon as David's successor over Israel; but*
■ *Solomon sinned, and God had to "humble*
■ *David's descendants" (11:39) by dividing the*
■ *nation into two kingdoms. The ten tribes of*
■ *the Northern Kingdom retain the name*
■ *Israel. The Southern Kingdom takes the*
■ *name of its dominant tribe, Judah.*

The structure of Kings is built upon a fixed framework having introductory and concluding formulas about each king's reign. The structure deviates from this framework with the inclusion of the Elijah and Elisha narrative cycles. The "deviation" points to the force of the prophets as shapers of the history of God's people.

1 Kings 1–2. This section completes the succession story of David begun in 2 Samuel 9–20. It depicts the ruthless struggle for power between Adonijah and Solomon as David neared his death. Only God's providential grace preserved the throne intact.

Background. The title "Kings" reflects the content of 1 and 2 Kings, which trace the history of God's covenant people under Israel's kings. Like the books of Samuel, 1 and 2 Kings were one book in the Hebrew tradition. The division of the book first occurred in the Greek version, which translated Samuel and Kings as four consecutive books entitled "First–Fourth Kingdoms."

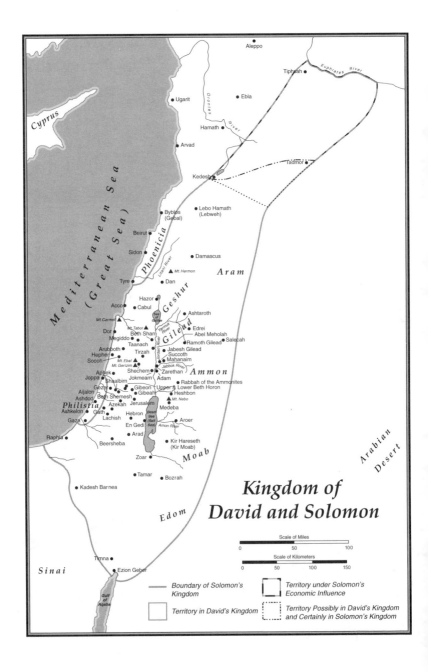

Kingdom of David and Solomon

1 Kings 3–11. The second section of the book concerns Solomon's reign. It focuses on the wisdom he received from the Lord (chaps. 3–4). He is able to assemble an impressive administration and to undertake numerous building projects, in particular the Jerusalem temple (chaps. 5–8). He becomes an important international figure through wealth, trade, and politics (chaps. 9–10). These accomplishments are God's blessing because of His covenant with David. But the author also tells how Solomon's apostasy (chap. 11) causes Israel to lose all he had achieved.

1 Kings 12–16. The book describes the period of antagonism between the two kingdoms of Israel and Judah. Jeroboam's revolt fulfilled God's judgment on Solomon's kingdom (chap. 12). Jeroboam's dynasty was condemned and usurped for its evil idolatry (chaps. 13–14). Israel suffered the bloodshed of war and political coups (chaps. 15–16). In all, nine dynasties ruled Israel in its two hundred years (931–722 B.C.). The kingdom of Judah enjoyed the stability of only one dynastic house since the Lord preserved the throne of David. Yet its kings also committed the idolatrous sins of their northern counterparts. The kings of Judah continually experienced war, and only righteous Asa had a long, prosperous rule (chaps. 14–15).

1 Kings 17–22. The account of Elijah and Elisha departs from the stereotyped reporting of the kings in chapters 12–16. Not only do kings make history, but these two prophets also dramatically shape the future of each royal house. Elijah's ministry occurs during Israel's greatest religious crisis under Ahab (chaps. 17–19) and Ahaziah (1 Kings 22:51–2 Kings 1:18). Ahab's reign declines because of wars with Aram and his theft of Naboth's vineyard (chaps. 20–22).

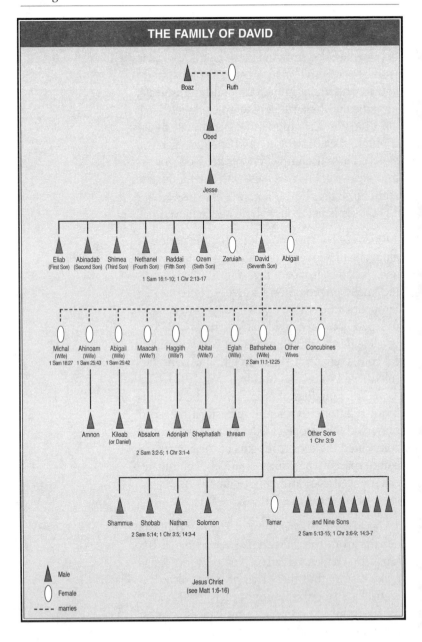

2 KINGS

- *Second Kings in a Nutshell: God destroys the*
- *kingdoms of Israel and Judah because their*
- *kings led the people to do evil by disobeying*
- *the covenant of the Lord (22:13).*

2 Kings 1–8. The introductory section continues the story of the prophets, Elijah and Elisha, who delivered the word of the Lord during this decadent period in the life of the nation. Elijah's ministry closes with his ascent to heaven.

But his successor, Elisha, picks up his mantle and performs a double portion of God's wondrous acts (chaps. 1–2). Through the prophetic ministry of Elisha, the Lord guides Israel to victories over their enemies, the Moabites and Arameans (chaps. 3; 6–7). God shows through Elisha that He also is the Lord of all nations who shapes their destinies (chaps. 5; 8). While the Lord meets the specific needs of His faithful people (chap. 4), He judges the servant Gehazi for his greed (5:19–27).

2 Kings 9–17. The second section describes the deterioration and eventual collapse of the northern state of Israel under the weight of its religious paganism and political infighting.

Jehu's dynasty rids Israel of its Baalism, postponing God's wrath. But the slide to destruction comes quickly afterwards with the rise and fall of four dynasties within the short span of thirty years. The climax of the account is the final chapter of the section, which explains why Israel did not survive (17:7–41). By disregarding the covenant, Israel chooses death (Deut. 30:19–20).

"Today I have given you the choice between life and death, between blessings and curses. I call on heaven and earth to witness the choice you make. Oh, that you would choose life, that you and your descendants might live! Choose to love the LORD your God and to obey him and commit yourself to him, for he is your life. Then you will live long in the land the LORD swore to give your ancestors Abraham, Isaac, and Jacob" (Deut. 30:19–20, NLT).

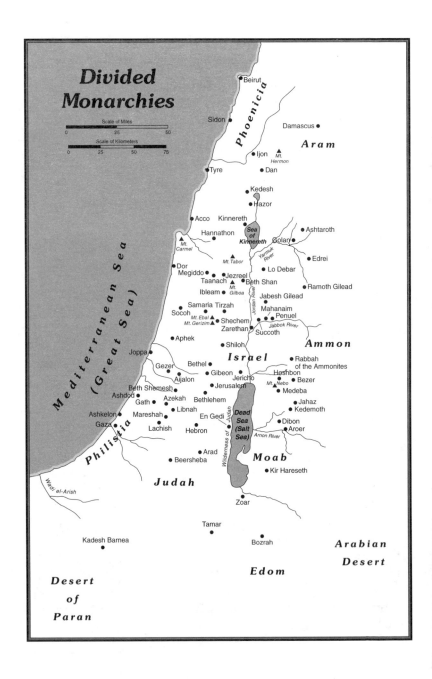

Divided
Monarchies

Scale of Miles
0   25   50

Scale of Kilometers
0   25   50   75

RULERS OF ISRAEL AND JUDAH

RULERS OF THE UNITED KINGDOM

Saul 1 Sam 9:1–31:13
David 1 Sam 16:1–1 Kgs 2:11
Solomon 1 Kgs 1:1–11:43

RULERS OF THE DIVIDED KINGDOM

RULERS OF ISRAEL		RULERS OF JUDAH	
Jeroboam I	I Kgs 11:26—14:20	Rehoboam	1 Kgs 11:42–14:31
		Abijah (Abijam)	1 Kgs 14:31–15:8
Nadab	1 Kgs 15:25-28	Asa	1 Kgs 15:8-24
Baasha	1 Kgs 15:27—16:7		
Elah	1 Kgs 16:6-14		
Zimri	1 Kgs 16:9-20		
Omri	1 Kgs 16:15-28		
Ahab	1 Kgs 16:28—22:40	Jehoshaphat	1 Kgs 22:41-50
Ahaziah	1 Kgs 22:40—2 Kgs 1:18	Jehoram	2 Kgs 8:16-24
Jehoram (Joram)	2 Kgs 1:17—9:26	Ahaziah	2 Kgs 8:24–9:29
Jehu	2 Kgs 9:1-10:36	Athaliah	2 Kgs 11:1-20
Jehoahaz	2 Kgs 13:1-9	Joash	2 Kgs 11:1–12:21
Jehoash (Joash)	2 Kgs 13:10—14:16	Amaziah	2 Kgs 14:1-20
Jeroboam II	2 Kgs 14:23-29	Azariah (Uzziah)	2 Kgs 14:21; 15:1-7
Zechariah	2 Kgs 14:29–15:12		
Shallum	2 Kgs 15:10-15	Jotham	2 Kgs 15:32-38
Menahem	2 Kgs 15:14-22		
Pekahiah	2 Kgs 15:22-26		
Pekah	2 Kgs 15:25-31	Ahaz (Jehoahaz)	2 Kgs 16:1-20
Hoshea	2 Kgs 15:30—17:6	Hezekiah	2 Kgs 18:1–20:21
		Manasseh	2 Kgs 21:1-18
		Amon	2 Kgs 21:19-26
		Josiah	2 Kgs 21:26–23:30
		Jehoahaz II (Shallum)	2 Kgs 23:30-33
		Jehoiakim (Eliakim)	2 Kgs 23:34–24:5
		Jehoiachin (Jeconiah)	2 Kgs 24:6-16; 25:27-30
		Zedekiah (Mattaniah)	2 Kgs 24:17–25:7

Meanwhile, the descendants of David escape annihilation only by the grace of God. The alliances of Jehoshaphat with Israelite kings (1 Kings 22; 2 Kings 2; 3; 2 Chron. 20:35–37), sealed by intermarriage (2 Kings 8:18; 2 Chron. 18:1), threaten the very existence of the Davidic line when Athaliah becomes queen mother. The salvation of Judah by Joash and the success of Amaziah's reign are the only two periods of stability in the otherwise tottering kingdom to the south.

2 Kings 18–25. This final section of Kings traces the survival of Judah after Samaria's collapse. From the perspective of the biblical writer, the reigns of Hezekiah (chaps. 18–20) and Josiah (chaps. 22–23) bring sweeping moral and religious reforms that prolong Judah's existence for another hundred years. However, this period also sees Judah's most wicked king, Manasseh (chap. 21). Because of Manasseh's heinous sins, Jerusalem falls under God's final judgment of expulsion (chaps. 24–25).

1 CHRONICLES

■ *First Chronicles in a Nutshell: God promises*
■ *David an eternal throne, choosing David to*
■ *found the true center of worship in Jerusalem*
■ *and appointing Solomon to build His Temple*
■ *(28:4–7).*

Differences with Samuel and Kings. While Chronicles shows a dependence on the books of Samuel and Kings, there are remarkable differences in content and theological perspective.

1. Chronicles was not written to supplement these former works, nor was it sim-

Background. Like the books of Samuel and Kings, 1 and 2 Chronicles were originally one book. The Hebrew title means the "chronological events of the period." The Greek version, which divided Chronicles into two books, entitled them "The Things Left Out" or "Omitted." This title reflects the misunderstanding that Chronicles was written to supplement the events left out of Samuel and Kings. The English name is derived from the Latin Vulgate's title, "The Chronicle of the Whole Sacred History."

ply a rewriting. These books offer a fresh
interpretation of Israel's monarchy. Samuel and Kings address the exilic community and explain why Israel's monarchy
failed. Chronicles addresses the restored
community and explains that God still
has a purpose for Israel. Chronicles was
written from a priestly perspective,
whereas Samuel and Kings were written
from a prophetic perspective.

2. Chronicles attempts a comprehensive
history, beginning with Adam, but Samuel and Kings are limited to the time of
the monarchy. In the book of Kings,
Judah still awaits release from captivity,
but Chronicles ends with the decree of
Cyrus anticipating Judah's return.

3. Chronicles features David and the kings
of Judah and avoids commenting on the
Northern Kingdom. Even the reign of
Saul is treated as a preamble to David's
accession. Chronicles tells the positive
contributions of David and Solomon and
omits unflattering events in their reigns.

4. The palace is center stage in Samuel and
Kings, but the Temple is central in
Chronicles. For the chronicler, the last-
ing contribution of the kings was religious. Samuel and Kings condemn sin
and urge repentance, but Chronicles
encourages the faithful to make a new
start.

1 Chronicles 1–9. The genealogies are not a ster-
ile recitation of names. They are a significant
statement of Israel's place in the whole sweep of
God's plan for the world. The chronicler founds
the proper appreciation of universal history in
the founding of Israel, the appointment of
David, and the building of the Temple, where

God resides in the world (a foretaste of the true Temple, Jesus Christ, who resides in the world as a man; see John 1–2).

1 Chronicles 10–20. The episode of Saul's death provides the background for David's kingdom (chap. 10). David's rule is glorious (chaps. 11–12), and the pinnacle of his reign is the bringing of the ark into Jerusalem (chaps. 13–16). God honors David's desire to build a temple by granting him an eternal throne (chap. 17). David prospers all the more because of God's blessing and dedicates to the Lord the spoils of his victories (chaps. 18–20).

1 Chronicles 21–29. The final section features the preparations David made for the building of the Temple. For the chronicler this is the most important contribution of the king and predominates his account of David's reign. The Temple site is divinely chosen (chaps. 21–22). David organizes the Levites and priests for the Temple work (chaps. 23–26), organizes the army (chap. 27), and holds a national convocation. There the people contribute gifts, and David appoints Solomon king and Zadok priest.

Background. First and Second Chronicles are one continuous narrative. Second Chronicles describes the construction of the Solomonic Temple and the religious life of the nation under Judah's kings.

2 CHRONICLES

- *Second Chronicles in a Nutshell: God dwells*
- *in His holy Temple and is faithful to His*
- *promise to redeem Israel (7:12).*

2 Chronicles 1–9. The introductory section is occupied with the Temple and Solomon's role in its construction (chaps. 1–7). The splendor of Solomon's kingdom is evidence for the chronicler that Solomon as David's son is the recipient of God's covenant promises (chaps. 8–9).

2 Chronicles 10–36. The second section of the book reviews the spiritual life of the nation under the kings of Judah during the divided monarchy. After the chronicler recounts the revolt of the northern tribes (chap. 10), his narrative alternates between periods of spiritual decay and religious reforms. He gives special consideration to the reformers Asa and Jehoshaphat (chaps. 14–20), Joash (chap. 24), Hezekiah (chaps. 29–32), and Josiah (chaps. 34–35). The final period of degeneracy is the last days of Judah's kings (36:1–13).

EZRA

- ■ *Ezra in a Nutshell: God uses pagan kings*
- ■ *and godly leaders to restore His people by*
- ■ *reinstituting Temple worship and reviving*
- ■ *the Law of Moses.*

The book of Ezra tells the history of the Jews' return from Babylon. It continues the story that Chronicles left unfinished.

Ezra 1–6. The first half of the book concerns the expedition ordered by King Cyrus (538 B.C.) to rebuild the Temple under Sheshbazzar of Judah. The book continues the theme of Temple and priesthood begun in Chronicles (Ezra 3:1–6, 10–11; 6:16–22). The importance of the Levites and priests to the community is evidenced by the careful cataloging of those who returned (2:36–54, 61–62). The Levites supervise the rebuilding of the Temple and are reorganized in time to officiate at the first Passover celebration (3:8–9; 6:16–20).

Ezra 7–10. The second half of the book concerns Ezra's ministry, which began fifty-eight

Background. The book of Ezra is named for the book's principle character. This scribe revived the Law of Moses as the basis for Jewish religious and social life during the period of restoration following the Babylonian Exile. In the Hebrew Bible, Ezra–Nehemiah is one book. It occurs in the third and final section (called the "Writings") and precedes Chronicles, which is the last book of the Hebrew Bible.

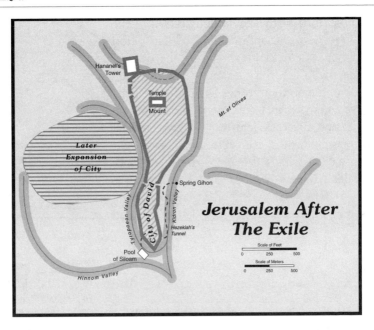

Jerusalem After The Exile

	Scale of Feet		
	0	250	500
	Scale of Meters		
	0	250	500

THE RETURN FROM EXILE

PHASE	DATE	SCRIPTURE REFERENCE	JEWISH LEADER	PERSIAN RULER	EXTENT OF THE RETURN	EVENTS OF THE RETURN
FIRST	538 B.C.	Ezra 1–6	Zerubbabel Jeshua	Cyrus	(1) Anyone who wanted to return could go. (2) The temple in Jerusalem was to be rebuilt. (3) Royal treasury provided funding of the temple rebuilding. (4) Gold and silver worship articles taken from temple by Nebuchadnezzar were returned.	(1) Burnt offerings were made. (2) The Feast of Tabernacles was celebrated. (3) The rebuilding of the temple was begun. (4) Persian ruler ordered rebuilding to be ceased. (5) Darius, King of Persia, ordered rebuilding to be resumed in 520 B.C. (6) Temple was completed and dedicated in 516 B.C.
SECOND	458 B.C.	Ezra 7–10	Ezra	Artaxerxes Longimanus	(1) Anyone who wanted to return could go. (2) Royal treasury provided funding. (3) Jewish civil magistrates and judges were allowed.	Men of Israel intermarried with foreign women.
THIRD	444 B.C.	Nehemiah 1–13	Nehemiah	Artaxerxes Longimanus	Rebuilding of wall of Jerusalem was allowed.	(1) Rebuilding of wall of Jerusalem was opposed by Sanballat the Horonite, Tobiah the Ammonite, and Geshem the Arab. (2) Rebuilding of wall was completed in 52 days. (3) Walls were dedicated. (4) Ezra read the Book of the Law to the people. (5) Nehemiah initiated reforms.

years (458 B.C.) after the completion of the Temple (515 B.C.). In the latter half of the book, the emphasis shifts to the Law of Moses. Ezra is commissioned to teach and establish the customs of Jewish law (7:11, 14, 25–26). Ezra is a learned scribe devoted to the Law (7:6, 10–12). He leads the people in a spiritual awakening that results in a covenant renewal (10:3).

NEHEMIAH

■ *Nehemiah in a Nutshell: God encircles His*
■ *people with protection by the walls Nehemiah*
■ *rebuilt and by the law Ezra reestablished.*

The majority of the book is Nehemiah's first-person memoirs (1:1–7:73; 12:27–13:31). Ezra's ministry is reported in the third person (Neh. 8:1–12:30).

Nehemiah 1–7. The book opens with Nehemiah's memoirs, which tell the governor's role in refortifying Jerusalem (chaps. 1–3). He reports the opposition he encounters from the Samaritans and shows how God has enabled him to succeed (chaps. 4–6). At God's prompting, Nehemiah takes steps to repopulate the city by reviewing those who had first returned (chap. 7).

Nehemiah 8–10. The account of Ezra's ministry is told in the third person. Ezra's proclamation of the Law begins on the first day of the seventh month (8:2) and continues probably each morning for one week. His reading of the Law encourages the exiles to rejoice and to celebrate the Feast of Tabernacles in the proper way (chap. 8). By hearing the Law, the people come under conviction, and collectively the nation recalls the evil of Israel's past (chap. 9). The

God's Word is trustworthy and essential for faith. It must be studied and heeded as the only authoritative rule for living. Ezra and Nehemiah make it transparently clear how important and essential God's truth is for God's people.

Background. The book of Nehemiah is named for its principal character. In the postexilic period Nehemiah refortified Jerusalem, established civil authority, and began religious reforms. Ezra–Nehemiah was one book in the Hebrew Bible until the fifteenth century A.D. The English versions follow the tradition of the Greek church fathers and Latin Old Testament by separating them.

result is a covenant renewal in which they pledge themselves to the Law (chap.10).

Nehemiah 11–13. The concluding section completes the themes already begun in chapters 1–10. The repopulation theme begun in chapter 7 continues with the catalog of new residents in Jerusalem to show a continuity with their ancestral faith and their hope in a new Israel (11:1–12:26). The dedication ceremonies of the walls (12:27–47) remind the reader of the opposition the Jews endured, yet the success they enjoyed because of God's good favor.

Finally, the variety of reforms introduced by Nehemiah enforced the features of the covenant undertaken by the community (13:1–31).

ESTHER

- *Esther in a Nutshell: God works behind the*
- *scenes to save the Jews from destruction by*
- *exalting Esther as queen of Persia and turn-*
- *ing the tables on their enemies (4:14; 9:11).*

Esther 1. The Persian King Ahasuerus (Xerxes in Greek) convenes a royal reception in his third year (483 B.C.) at Susa of Elam (modern southwestern Iran). The assembly Xerxes calls lasts for 180 days, during which he displays the splendor of his wealth. It culminates in a seven-day feast of luxurious dining and drunkenness. The opulence of the Persian court is described to indicate the vast resources and power of the king (1:4–9).

In a drunken stupor, the king calls for Queen Vashti to "display her beauty" before his guests (1:10–11). Her refusal, probably out of

Background. In the Greek and English versions, Esther is the last book in the collection of Historical Books. In the Hebrew arrangement of the Old Testament, the book is one of the five *Megilloth (rolls or scrolls)* occurring in the third and final section (the *Kethubhim* or *Writings)* of the Hebrew Bible. The book's plot includes the origins of the Jewish festival of Purim. Esther is traditionally read on that annual celebration (Adar 14 and 15).

decency, threatens the king's reputation. At Memucan's advice, the king deposes her (1:10–22). Xerxes' action is a parody on Persian might, for the powerful king could not command even his own wife.

Esther 2–3. The second section of the story concerns the exaltation of Esther (chap. 2) and the evil plot by Haman to exterminate the Jews (chap. 3). The role of Mordecai as Esther's cousin and Haman's hated enemy links the two episodes.

Esther 4–5. Esther's position enables her to save the Jews if she is willing to risk her own standing (chap. 4). After recounting Esther's vow of devotion, the author tells how Esther takes the lead and devises her own scheme to outmaneuver Haman. Ironically, Haman unwittingly devises his own end (chap. 5).

Positions of influence are opportunities to show loyalty to God and His purposes for His people.

Esther 6–7. This section features the key reversal in Haman's and Mordecai's fates. Mordecai is honored by the king, much to Haman's humiliation (chap. 6). The final indignity of foolish Haman is his pathetic effort to save himself from the gallows (chap. 7).

Esther 8–9. This royal decree Mordecai writes answers Haman's evil decree (3:8–11). This parallelism continues the theme of reversal, the decree enabling the Jews to take the offensive against their enemies (chap. 8). The thirteenth of Adar, the day planned for the Jews' destruction, is exchanged for the two-day celebration of Purim because of the Jews' conquest (chap. 9).

Esther 10. The story concludes in the way it began by describing the power and influence of Xerxes' kingdom. The author refers the reader to the official records of the empire where a full

God works in all history even when His actions are not obvious and when He does not raise up a prophet to interpret His actions.

account of the kingdom and the role played by Mordecai can be examined (10:1–2; 1 Kings 14:19; 15:7). Mordecai contributes to the prosperity of the empire and cares for the Jews' welfare (10:3). The greatness of Mordecai vindicates the Jews as a people. Their heritage is not a threat to the Gentiles, but rather through Mordecai and the Jews the empire enjoys peace.

THE POETIC AND WISDOM BOOKS

- The Word of God, as it has come to us
- through the experiences of the people of God,
- expresses all the emotions of the life of faith,
- and it deals with many areas of experience
- that might seem mundane and unspiritual.

- This is nowhere more true than in its poetic
- and wisdom literature. The Psalms express
- every emotion the believer encounters in life,
- be it praise and love for God, anger at those
- who practice violence and deceit, personal
- grief and confusion, or appreciation for
- God's truth. Proverbs not only examines
- moral issues, but it also helps us deal with
- the ordinary matters of life, such as indebt-
- edness and work habits. Song of Solomon
- celebrates the joy of love between man and
- woman. Job and Ecclesiastes make us face
- our most profound questions and thereby
- bring us to a more genuine faith in God. In
- sum, all these books deal with real life.

- Traditionally, we speak of Psalms and Song
- of Solomon as being the books of biblical
- poetry and Job, Proverbs, and Ecclesiastes as
- biblical wisdom. These books will be the
- focus of this section. The five books of Job,
- Psalms, Proverbs, Ecclesiastes, and Song of
- Solomon give us the best examples of how
- biblical hymns, songs, proverbs, and reflec-
- tions are to be read.

JOB

■ *Job in a Nutshell: The book of Job tells of a*
■ *righteous man whom God, at Satan's insis-*
■ *tence, afflicts as a test of his fidelity and*
■ *integrity. Though Job is a righteous man,*
■ *Gods allows Satan to test him through per-*
■ *sonal loss and physical pain. Puzzled, then*
■ *angered, by his predicament, Job lashes out*
■ *at God. Shocked at his attitude, Job's friends*
■ *rebuke him and demand his repentance.*
■ *Undaunted, Job seeks an audience with God,*
■ *which he receives. Finally God confronts Job,*
■ *who can then only prostrate himself and*
■ *repent. God restores Job's fortunes and*
■ *declares him to be more righteous than his*
■ *friends.*

Background. The book itself does not give any indication of the time it was written. Traditionally the date has been placed during the time of the patriarchs or during the time of Solomon.

Job 1:1–2:13. In 1:1, Job is declared to have been altogether upright and blameless. At the very outset, therefore, the possibility that his sufferings might be punishment or discipline is thrown out of court.

Satan (meaning "adversary" or "accuser") appears before God in 1:6 and challenges the validity of Job's piety. He poses the central question of the book: "Does Job fear God for nothing?" (1:9).

God then allows Satan to test Job by bringing into his life loss of material goods, all of his children, and his health.

Job 3–31. Job dialogues with three friends (Eliphaz, Bildad, and Zophar), who come to comfort him but are horrified at his anger at God. They try without success to persuade him to repent of some sin. Job concludes this dialogue with a monologue in which he laments his fate but continues to protest his innocence.

Job 32–37. A fifth speaker, Elihu, tries to make sense of the situation and to point out Job's error.

Job 38–42:6. Job seeks an audience with God, which he receives. Finally, God confronts Job in a divine speech that falls into two parts: 38:2–40:2 and 40:7–41:34. Job can then only prostrate himself and repent.

Job 42:7–17. God restores Job's fortunes and declares him to be more righteous than his friends (chap. 42).

PSALMS

■ *Psalms in a Nutshell: The book of Psalms or*
■ *the Psalter is the hymnal of Israelite worship*
■ *and the Bible's book of personal devotions. In*
■ *it we not only find expression of all the emo-*
■ *tions of life but also some of the most pro-*
■ *found teaching in the entire Scripture.*

The word *psalms* comes from the Greek translation of the Old Testament and refers primarily to stringed instruments and then secondarily to songs sung to stringed instruments.

The Compilation of the Psalms. Psalms divides into five sections or "books": (1) Psalms 1–41; (2) Psalms 42–72; (3) Psalms 73–89; (4) Psalms 90–106; (5) Psalms 107–150. Old Testament scholar John Walton believes the classification of the Psalms shows, over time, Israel's relationship with the covenant. The first two psalms express God's love for righteousness and His covenant with David.

Psalms 3–41 grow out of David's conflict with Saul. Psalms 42–72 celebrate David's reign. Psalms 90–106 reflect on the temple's destruction. Psalms 107–145 look forward to the

THE CHARACTERISTICS OF GOD PRESENTED IN THE PSALMS	
CHARACTERISTICS	**SELECTED PASSAGES**
Anger	5:6; 6:1; 27:9; 30:5; 73:20; 76:7,10; 89:38; 103:8; 106:29,32,40; 108:11; 145:8
Avenger	9:12; 24:5; 26:1; 53:5; 58:6; 59:4; 68:21-25; 72:4; 86:17; 112:8; 139:19
Creator	8:3; 24:2; 78:69; 86:9; 93:1; 95:4; 96:5; 119:73, 90–91; 121:2; 124:8; 136:5-9
Deliverer (Savior)	7:1,10; 9:14; 24:5; 27:9; 37:39; 39:8; 71:2; 80:2; 119:41, 94, 123,146, 173; 132:16
Faithful	40:10; 54:5; 91:4; 92:2; 94:14; 98:3; 100:5; 115:1; 119:75; 143:1
Forgiving	25:11; 32:5; 65:3; 78:38; 79:9; 85:2; 86:5; 99:8; 103:3,12; 130:3-4
Glory	8:1; 24:7; 26:8; 29:1; 63:2; 66:2; 79:9; 89:17; 97:6; 106:20; 113:4; 115:1; 138:5
Good	13:6; 25:7; 27:13; 31:19; 34:8; 73:1; 86:5,17; 100:5; 106:1; 119:65, 68; 125:4; 145:7,9
Gracious	67:1; 86:15; 103:8; 111:4; 112:4; 116:5; 119:58; 145:8
Healer	6:2; 30:2; 103:3; 107:20; 147:3
Holy	20:6; 22:3; 29:2; 30:4; 68:5,35; 71:22; 77:13; 78:41; 89:18,35; 99:3,5,9
Jealous	78:58; 79:5
Judge	7:8,11; 9:4,7-8; 50:4,6; 75:2,7; 98:9; 103:6; 110:6
Justice	7:6; 9:8,16; 33:5; 36:6; 67:4; 96:10; 99:4; 101:1; 103:6; 140:12
King	5:2; 9:7; 11:4; 44:4; 47:2-9; 66:7; 68:16,24; 74:12; 89:14; 96:10; 97:1; 145:1,11-13
Living	18:46; 42:2; 84:2

THE CHARACTERISTICS OF GOD PRESENTED IN THE PSALMS	
CHARACTERISTICS	**SELECTED PASSAGES**
Love	6:4; 21:7; 25:6; 47:4; 48:9; 52:8; 60:5; 62:12; 66:20; 98:3; 103:4, 8, 11, 17; 106:1, 45; 117:2; 119:41, 64
Majesty	8:1; 68:34; 76:4; 93:1; 96:6; 104:1; 111:3; 145:5
Mercy	4:1; 5:7; 9:13; 26:11; 30:10; 31:9; 41:4,10; 57:1; 78:38; 116:1
Only God	18:31; 35:10; 73:25; 95:3; 96:4-5; 97:7; 113:5; 135:5
Perfect	18:30; 92:15
Present	16:11; 23:4; 35:22; 38:21; 48:3; 73:23; 89:15; 105:4; 110:5; 114:7; 139:7-12
Protector	3:3; 5:11; 7:10; 33:20; 66:9; 97:10; 115:9; 127:1; 145:20
Provider	67:6; 68:9; 78:23-29; 81:16; 85:12; 107:9, 35-38; 132:15; 136:25; 144:12-15; 145:15
Redeemer	19:14; 25:22; 107:2; 119:134,154; 130:8
Refuge, Rock	7:1; 14:6; 19:14; 27:1; 28:1; 42:9; 62:1, 8; 73:28; 89:26; 91:2, 9; 92:15; 118:8
Repent	90:13; 106:45
Righteousness	4:1; 11:7; 36:6; 50:6; 72:1; 89:14; 96:13; 111:3; 119:40; 129:4
Shepherd	23:1; 28:9; 74:1; 77:20; 78:52; 79:13; 80:1; 95:7; 100:3
Spirit	51:11; 104:30; 139:7; 143:10
Universal	24:1; 50:1,12; 59:13; 65:2, 5; 66:4; 68:32; 69:34; 86:9; 96:1, 7; 99:2-3; 100:1; 138:4; 150:6
Wisdom	104:24; 136:5; 147:5
Wonder Worker	40:5; 46:8; 65:5; 66:3, 5; 68:7-8; 72:18; 73:28; 74:13; 78:4; 81:10; 86:8, 10; 98:1; 107:8, 15; 135:8-9; 136:4, 10-16; 145:4

HUMAN CHARACTERISTICS PRESENTED IN THE PSALMS	
CHARACTERISTICS	**SELECTED PASSAGES**
Afflicted, Poor, Needy	12:5; 14:6; 22:26; 25:16; 34:2, 6; 49:2; 68:5, 10; 72:2; 74:19; 76:9; 82:3; 113:7; 136:23; 145:14
Anger	37:8; 124:3; 138:7; 139:21-22
Blessed	1:1; 2:12; 3:8; 5:12; 24:5; 34:8; 41:1; 65:4; 84:4, 12; 106:3; 119:1; 129:8; 132:15; 134:3
Confident	3:5; 4:8; 27:1; 30:6; 41:11; 71:5
Covenant/Partners	25:10; 50:5,16; 74:20; 78:10, 37; 89:3, 28, 34, 39; 103:18; 105:8; 106:45; 111:5, 9; 132:12
Death/Sheol	6:5; 16:10; 23:4; 31:17; 44:22; 49:9-20; 55:4,15, 23; 68:20; 78:33, 50; 82:7; 103:15; 104:29; 115:17
Enemies	3:1, 7; 4:2; 6:10; 8:2; 9:3; 18:37, 48; 27:2; 41:2, 7; 66:3; 68:1, 21; 78:53, 61, 66; 81:14; 108:12; 129:1; 132:18
Faithful, Godly	4:3; 18:25; 26:1; 31:23; 37:28; 73:1; 84:11; 85:10-11; 86:2; 97:10; 101:2; 108:1; 125:4; 139:23-24
Fool, Impious	14:1; 53:1; 74:18, 22; 92:6; 94:8; 107:17
Humans, Mortal	22:6; 33:13; 49:7; 55:13; 56:4; 62:9; 82:5; 89:47; 115:16; 133:1; 139:16; 146:3
Joy	4:7; 16:9; 20:5; 21:1; 27:6; 28:7; 34:2; 47:1; 48:11; 53:6; 63:11; 68:3; 81:1; 90:14; 98:4; 100:1; 107:22; 145:7

HUMAN CHARACTERISTICS PRESENTED IN THE PSALMS

CHARACTERISTICS	SELECTED PASSAGES
King of Israel/ Anointed	2:2, 6-8; 20:6; 28:8; 45:1-9; 61:6; 63:11; 78:70; 84:9; 92:10; 122:5; 144:10
Kings of Earth	33:16; 48:4; 68:12; 76:12; 94:20; 102:15; 106:41; 110:5; 119:23, 46, 161; 138:4; 146:3; 149:8
Loving God	5:11; 18:1; 69:36; 70:4; 91:14; 97:10; 116:1; 119:132; 145:20
Nations/Peoples	9:5, 15, 19; 22:27; 44:11; 46:6; 59:5; 67:2; 68:30; 72:17; 78:55; 82:8; 99:1-2; 105:1,13; 110:6
Righteous	5:12; 11:5; 14:5; 15:2; 17:1,15; 18:20; 23:3; 33:1; 34:15; 37:6, 12, 16, 21, 25, 30; 55:22; 58:10; 68:3; 72:2; 92:12; 97:11; 106:31; 125:3; 142:7; 146:8
Sacrifice	4:5; 51:16, 19; 107:22
Sin	5:10; 14:3; 19:13; 25:7; 36:1-2; 51:1, 5, 13; 52:2; 58:3; 66:18; 68:21; 89:32; 99:8; 103:10, 12; 106:6, 13-39, 43; 107:11, 17
Suffering/Afflicted	22:24; 31:7; 38:3; 41:3; 55:3; 119:50, 107, 153
Trust	4:5; 9:10; 13:5; 20:7; 21:7; 22:4, 9; 28:7; 37:3; 40:3; 52:8; 62:8; 84:12; 112:7; 115:9; 116:10; 125:1
Wicked	5:4; 6:8; 7:9,14; 11:2; 23:4; 26:5; 27:2; 32:10; 52:1; 53:1, 4; 55:3; 58:3; 59:2; 68:2; 73:3; 82:4; 84:10; 94:3,13,16,23; 104:35; 107:34, 42; 119:53, 95, 119, 150, 155; 147:6
Wisdom	90:12; 107:43; 111:10; 119:98

return of worship in Jerusalem. Psalms 146–150 command Israel to praise God.

Types of Psalms. When studying a psalm, one should consider the following questions: (1) Was it sung by an individual or the congregation? (2) What was the psalm's purpose (praise, cry for help, thanksgiving, admonition)? (3) Does it mention any special themes, such as the king and the royal house, or Zion? By asking these questions, scholars have identified a number of psalm types.

PROVERBS

■ *Proverbs in a Nutshell: Proverbs is a collec-*
■ *tion of wise counsel for living well.*

In Proverbs, wisdom begins with God; His centrality is assumed throughout. Wise people are those who know God, trust Him, and behave toward others according to God's principles. Attitudes and actions have consequences, and these are spelled out in short, pithy, unforgettable sayings.

The Hebrew word translated *proverb* has a broader meaning than does the English word. This word probably means "to rule" or "to be like." A proverb is a snapshot from life that shows us what life is like.

Proverbs 1:1-7. Introduction. This collection is introduced as the proverbs of Solomon. These proverbs have a goal of instructing youth in understanding, judgment, and wise behavior. The foundation for human wisdom is fear of the Lord.

"The fear of the LORD is the beginning of knowledge, but fools despise wisdom and discipline" (Prov. 1:7).

Proverbs 1: 8 – 2:22. Two Types of Human Beings. Youth are encouraged to give attention to the teaching of their parents and to avoid the temptations to follow peers who want quick gain at any price. There are two classes of human beings: those who seek to live by wisdom and those who despise wisdom. The consequences of these two approaches to life are easy to see.

Proverbs 3:1 –4:27. Trust God. One's relationship with God is key to life at its best. God's wisdom is woven into the very fabric of creation. But there are many who fail to live in accordance with God's ways. Beware of such people. Keep you eye on God and His ways.

Proverbs 5:1 –7:27. Avoid Sexual Sin. Sexuality is a gift from God and is a great blessing, provided God's ways are followed. Temptation to sexual sin is powerful. Counter it by remembering the tragic consequences of yielding to it.

Proverbs 8:1–9:18. Wisdom's Invitation. Wisdom is an essential attribute of God and as such is displayed in the universe He has created. Wisdom and folly are in competition for the minds of men and women.

Proverbs 10:1–32. Work and Speech. Work and laziness have two quite different consequences. A wise person will learn what to say and when to say it.

Proverbs 11: 1–31. Generosity and Greed. Material gain is a blessing but can be used for either good or ill.

Proverbs 12: 1–28. Truthfulness and Deceit. The wise are truthful and their speech brings healing. Fools are deceptive and destructive in their speech.

Proverbs 13: 1–25. The Disciplined Life. Habits and choice of companions will shape character.

Proverbs 14: 1–35. Rich and Poor. The rich have many friends; the poor have few. Having compassion on the poor honors God.

Proverbs 15: 1–33. Reproof and Correction. The wise learn from criticism. Fools don't profit from it.

Proverbs 16: 1–33. God's Sovereignty. Humans make plans, but God is sovereign over all and determines the outcomes of human planning.

Proverbs 17:1–19:29. Family and Relationships. The wise person will give much attention to relationships within the family and in the cultivation of authentic friendship.

"Flog a mocker, and
the simple will learn
prudence;
Rebuke a discerning
man, and he will gain
knowledge"
(Prov. 19:25).

Proverbs 20:1–22:16. Choices and Their Consequences. Drunkenness, dishonesty, and laziness are destructive. Honesty and doing right provide a strong foundation for individual lives and for a nation.

Proverbs 22:17–24:22. Thirty Sayings of the Wise. These sayings of the wise contain a number of proverbs on proper etiquette in the presence of the rich and powerful, with the warning that it is foolish to try to ingratiate yourself before such men.

Proverbs 24:23–34. Additional Sayings. This is a further collection of wise sayings. An example story on the danger of laziness appears in 24:30-34.

Proverbs 25:1–29:27. Hezekiah Collection. This collection gives counsel to those who related to the king and to government authorities. It also instructs in the matter of personal relationships, conflict management, and dealing with difficult people.

Proverbs 30:1–33. Sayings of Agur. These sayings are prefaced by an acknowledgement of the vast difference between God and His creatures and the accuracy and sufficiency of God's words.

Proverbs 31:1–31. Sayings of Lemuel. These are words taught to King Lemuel by his mother. She begins by giving counsel to him as a ruler. This is followed by one of the most quoted passages in the Bible—a description of an excellent wife (31:10–31).

These proverbs contain striking parallels to the Egyptian Teachings of Amenemope. Those proverbs differ in form from the Proverbs of Solomon in that they consist of four stanzas whereas the Proverbs of Solomon contain two part verses.

Background.
Ecclesiastes tells us it was written by a son of David who was king in Jerusalem over Israel (1:1, 12). This points to Solomon since he alone, after David, ruled both Judah and Israel. Solomon writes under the pen name *Qoheleth* or the Teacher.

"Here is my final conclusion: Fear God and obey his commands, for this is the duty of every person. God will judge us for everything we do, including every secret thing, whether good or bad" (Eccles. 12:13–14, NLT).

ECCLESIATES

■ *Ecclesiastes in a Nutshell: Ecclesiastes is an*
■ *unvarnished account of life after the fall of*
■ *man.*

Ecclesiastes 1:1–2. Verse 1 gives the title of the work, and verse 2 gives its theme. The word *vanity* or *meaningless* translates the Hebrew word *hebel*, which originally meant *breath.* From *breath* comes the idea of that which is insubstantial, transitory, and of fleeting value. For Ecclesiastes, anything that does not have eternal value has no real value. Everything in this world is fleeting and therefore, in the final analysis, pointless.

The teacher then examines those pursuits in which we seek permanence and security—wisdom (1:12–18) and wealth (2:1–11). He shows that in the face of death neither wisdom nor wealth is substantial. However, despite the fact that these pursuits are not permanently valuable, we should not reject them. Awareness of death can teach us to put all of these pursuits in perspective and to enjoy life as it is and not how we wish it would be.

The teacher concludes the book by placing life in God's perspective.

SONG OF SOLOMON

■ *Song of Solomon in a Nutshell: This is a song*
■ *that revolves around the first sexual union of*
■ *a married couple.*

Interpretation. No other book of the Bible (except perhaps Revelation) suffers under so many radically different interpretations as the Song of Solomon.

Like Ecclesiastes, Song of Solomon cannot be outlined in traditional ways. Also, it is not a drama but is best seen as a libretto for a musical.

The Song does have an internal structure. The second half of the Song mirrors the first half in reverse order. This is called a chiastic structure. At the center of the song the bride invites the bridegroom to enter her garden and he declares that he has entered (4:16–5:1).

Background. The full name of this book is "The Song of Songs, which is Solomon's." Often called Song of Solomon or, after the Latin, Canticles. The Hebrew idiom *Song of Songs* actually means *the best song.*

■ Traditionally the prophetic books are
■ divided into Major and Minor Prophets,
■ basically on the length of the books.

■ The books of the Major Prophets include Isa-
■ iah, Jeremiah, Lamentations, Ezekiel, and
■ Daniel. That Isaiah, Jeremiah, and Ezekiel
■ should be classified as major prophets should
■ be self-evident. All three were prominent fig-
■ ures in the history of Israel and have left us
■ with large collections of prophetic messages
■ and biographical materials. Isaiah minis-
■ tered in Judah from about 742 to 700 B.C. His
■ prophecy addresses issues facing his contem-
■ poraries as well as the situation of the future
■ exilic generation in Babylon. Jeremiah lived
■ in Judah during its final days prior to the fall
■ of Jerusalem in 586 B.C. After the fall of the
■ city, he was forced to accompany a group of
■ refugees to Egypt. His prophecy, while focus-
■ ing on contemporary events, also looks for-
■ ward to a time of restoration for God's
■ people. Ezekiel was an exile in Babylon
■ whose prophetic ministry took place between
■ 593 and 571 B.C. Like his counterparts Isa-
■ iah and Jeremiah, he prophesied both judg-
■ ment and restoration for God's people.

■ Lamentations has traditionally been attrib-
■ uted to Jeremiah and, in lamenting the city's
■ tragic destruction, focuses on an event that
■ occupied a great deal of Jeremiah's attention.
■ The book of Daniel, of course, contains sev-

- *eral prophecies of future events, though they*
- *are presented in an apocalyptic literary style*
- *that differs significantly from traditional*
- *prophetic forms.*

ISAIAH

- *Isaiah in a Nutshell: Israel's sin causes God*
- *to send Assyria to punish the people. Isaiah*
- *predicts the future Babylonian invasion as*
- *well. After their punishment, Israel will be*
- *redeemed by the coming son of David.*

Background. According to the book's heading, Isaiah prophesied from about 740 until about 700 B.C. during the reigns of the kings Uzziah, Jotham, Ahaz, and Hezekiah of Judah. Several New Testament passages appear to attribute the entire book to the prophet Isaiah (e.g., John 12:38–41).

Certainly the perspective of chapters 40–66 is much later than Isaiah's time, as the many references to the situations of the exiles, the naming of Cyrus of Persia, the exhortations to leave Babylon, and the description of ruined and uninhabited Jerusalem indicate. However, this need not mean that the author of the chapters lived in this later period. Isaiah could have projected himself into the future and addressed the exilic situation he knew God's people would eventually experience (compare 39:5–7). Though such a projection into the future would be unique among the writing prophets, at least on the scale proposed for Isaiah, it would be consistent with one of the major theological themes of the book's later chapters, namely, God's ability to predict events long before He actually brings them to pass.

God's ideal for His covenant people Israel will indeed be realized but only after His judgment purifies the covenant community of those who rebel against His authority. God sovereignly controls the destiny of nations but also demands loyalty from His people.

THE PROPHETS IN HISTORY
(9th—5th century B.C.)

Prophet	Approximate Dates (B.C.)	Location/ Home	Basic Bible Passage	Central Teaching	Key Verse
Elijah	875–850	Tishbe	1 Kgs 17:1–2 Kgs 2:18	Yahweh, not Baal, is God	1 Kgs 18:21
Micaiah	856	Samaria	1 Kgs 22; 2 Chr 18	Judgment on Ahab; proof of prophecy	1 Kgs 22:28
Elisha	855–800	Abel Meholah	1 Kgs 19:15-21; 2 Kgs 2–9; 13	God's miraculous power	2 Kgs 5:15
Jonah	786-746	Gath Hepher	2 Kgs 14:25; Jonah	God's universal concern	Jonah 4:11
Hosea	786-746	Israel	Hosea	God's unquenchable love	Hos 11:8-9
Amos	760-750	Tekoa	Amos	God's call for justice and righteousness	Amos 5:24
Isaiah	740–698	Jerusalem	2 Kgs 19–20; Isaiah	Hope through repentance and suffering	Isa 1:18; 53:4-6
Micah	735–710	Moresheth Gath Jerusalem	Jer 26:18; Micah	Call for humble mercy and justice	Mic 6:8
Oded	733	Samaria	2 Chr 28:9-11	Do not go beyond God's command	2 Chr 28:9
Nahum	686-612	Elkosh	Nahum	God's jealousy protects His people	Nah 1:2-3
Zephaniah	640-621	?	Zephaniah	Hope for the humble and righteous	Zeph 2:3
Jeremiah	626–584	Anathoth/ Jerusalem	2 Chr 36:12; Jeremiah	Faithful prophet points to new covenant	Jer 31:33-34
Huldah (the prophetess)	621	Jerusalem	2 Kgs 22; 2 Chr 34	God's Book is accurate	2 Kgs 22:16
Habakkuk	608-598	?	Habakkuk	God calls for faithfulness	Hab 2:4
Ezekiel	593–571	Babylon	Ezekiel	Future hope for new community of worship	Ezek 37:12-13
Obadiah	580	Jerusalem	Obadiah	Doom on Edom to bring God's kingdom	Obad 21
Joel	539-531	Jerusalem	Joel	Call to repent and experience God's Spirit	Joel 2:28-29
Haggai	520	Jerusalem	Ezra 5:1; 6:14; Haggai	The priority of God's house	Hag 2:8-9
Zechariah	520-514	Jerusalem	Ezra 5:1; 6:14; Zechariah	Faithfulness will lead to God's universal rule	Zech 14:9
Malachi	500-450	Jerusalem	Malachi	Honor God and wait for His righteousness	Mal 4:2

Isaiah 1–12. Israel has broken her covenant with the Lord. He will first send warnings. Then God will bring judgment through Israel's enemies. Third, He promises a leader—a righteous son of David who alone can rebuild the nation.

Isaiah 13–27. These chapters contain a series of judgment speeches against various nations of Isaiah's day (chaps. 13–23) and pave the way for the message of universal judgment (chaps. 24–27). These judgment speeches serve as a reminder to God's people of His absolute sovereignty over all nations, including both their enemies and allies. God's people need not fear the surrounding nations or rely on their aid.

Isaiah 28–35. The theme of this section is judgment and hope for Judah. Much of this material, which contains several woe oracles (28:1; 29:1, 15; 30:1; 31:1; 33:1), is accusatory and threatening, but these chapters also contain words of hope. Rebellious Judah must reject the example of the Northern Kingdom and resist the temptation to rely on foreign alliances. Instead the nations must trust in God alone as the One who is sovereign over the destiny of His people and of the surrounding nations.

Isaiah 36–39. These chapters record significant events during the reign of Hezekiah. They repeat 2 Kings 18–20 in many respects, recording three significant events of Hezekiah's reign: (1) the Lord's miraculous deliverance of Jerusalem and the destruction of the Assyrians; (2) Hezekiah's recovery from a serious illness; and (3) Hezekiah's unwise dealings with the messengers from Babylon. Isaiah played a prominent role in these events, each of which prompted at least one prophetic oracle.

The chapters are not in chronological order. The Assyrian deliverance (chaps. 36–37) followed the events recorded in chapters 38–39. Perhaps chapter 39 comes last because its reference to Babylon provides a frame for chapters 13–39. Also, by showing that even godly Hezekiah had his faults and ultimately could not prevent Judah's downfall, it paves the way for chapters 40–66, the setting of which is the Babylonian captivity.

"The future is as bright as the promises of God"—William Carey.

Isaiah 40–48. This section addresses the deliverance of the exiles from Babylon. God emphasizes that He is both willing and able to deliver His exiled people. Much of the section focuses on God's superiority to the nations and their idols.

Isaiah 49–55. This passage deals with the restoration of Jerusalem. Chapters 41–42 introduced Cyrus and the Lord's ideal servant as important instruments in God's program for Israel's redemption. Chapters 43–48 focused on Cyrus's role, while chapters 49–55 develop in more detail the ideal servant's part in the drama. This section is arranged in three panels (49:1–50:3; 50:4–52; 52:13–54:17), each of which begins with a servant song followed by an encouraging message for personified Jerusalem. A moving call to covenantal renewal concludes the section (55:1–13).

"But he was wounded and crushed for our sins. He was beaten that we might have peace. He was whipped, and we were healed!" (Isa. 53:5, NLT).

Isaiah 56–66. Despite God's promise of a new era of blessing and His invitation to reconciliation, the reality of Israel's rebellious spirit remained. Isaiah 56–66 indicates that only the repentant would participate in the new era. Those who followed the sinful ways of earlier generations would be excluded. Though many of the promises of chapters 40–55 are reiterated here, the theme of God's purifying, discriminating judgment is also prominent.

JEREMIAH

- *Jeremiah in a Nutshell: God led Jeremiah to*
- *preach treason to a weak, unfaithful people.*
- *This came after many warnings. God was*
- *using Babylon to punish Judah for their*
- *devotion to idols. Judah faced a choice.*
- *They were considering a defense treaty with*
- *Egypt or surrender to the Babylonians. Jer-*
- *emiah urged the latter as God's direction*
- *and suffered the consequences for being*
- *God's prophet.*

Background. According to the book's heading, Jeremiah was a priest from Anathoth whose prophetic career began in the thirteenth year of Josiah (627–626 B.C.) and continued until the final exile of Judah in 586. Chapters 39–44 indicate that Jeremiah continued to minister after the fall of Jerusalem and was forced to accompany a group of exiles to Egypt.

Jeremiah focuses on Judah's forsaking their covenant with God who loved them.

Jeremiah 1. God calls Jeremiah.

Jeremiah 2:1–24:10. These chapters contain several judgment oracles against God's people, as well as many of the prophet's emotionally charged prayers to and dialogues with the Lord. The major theme of the section is sinful Judah's coming downfall, yet glimpses of future restoration also appear.

"Before I formed you in the womb I knew you, before you were born I set you apart; I appointed you as a prophet to the nations" (Jer. 1:5).

Jeremiah 25–51. These chapters outline God's future program in detail. The theme of judgment upon Judah, introduced in chapters 1–24, is developed. This section also describes divine judgment on a universal scale, as well as the future restoration of God's people. The theme of universal judgment begins (chap. 25) and ends (chaps. 46–51) this section, with the downfall of Babylon being highlighted (25:12–14, 26; 50–51).

Background. Though it does not identify its author, tradition has ascribed the book of Lamentations to Jeremiah. The author of the book, like the prophet, was an eyewitness of Jerusalem's fall and displayed great emotion in his prayers to God. The book was written between the destruction of the city in 586 B.C. and the rebuilding of the Temple seventy years later.

Jeremiah 52. This chapter is parallel to 2 Kings 24:18–25:30. It gives a detailed account of Jerusalem's fall to the Babylonians.

LAMENTATIONS

- *Lamentations in a Nutshell: The author*
- *laments the fall of Jerusalem. While*
- *acknowledging that the calamity was*
- *deserved, he longs for God to restore His*
- *favor.*

The book contains five poems, corresponding to the chapter divisions. The central poem is sixty-six verses in length, while the others contain twenty-two verses each. All but the last poem are acrostics, in which the form reflects the successive letters of the Hebrew alphabet.

Lamentations 1. Jerusalem had once been a queen; now she is a slave. In desperation she confesses her sin and asks the Lord to consider her anguish.

Lamentations 2. The Lord attacks Jerusalem as if she were His enemy. Rather than protecting the city with His powerful right hand, He turns His might against her and pours His angry judgment upon her like fire.

"Because of the LORD's great love we are not consumed, for his compassions never fail. They are new every morning; great is your faithfulness" (Lam. 3:22–23).

Lamentations. 3. Despite experiencing the Lord's disfavor, the author retains hope. The Lord is sovereign and decrees both calamity and blessing. The author urges his compatriots to acknowledge their sins and come before the Lord with a repentant spirit.

Lamentations 4. As the city's children cry out in hunger and thirst, no one takes pity on them. The once robust princes are shriveled up from lack of food. Starving mothers who used to be filled with compassion even eat their own children.

Lamentations 5. This chapter is a prayer for restoration. After asking the Lord to take note of His people's disgrace, the author describes their plight in detail to motivate God to respond in mercy. In a final burst of energy (vv. 19–22), the author praises God as the eternal King, asks how long they have to suffer rejection, and prays that God might restore and renew His relationship with His people.

EZEKIEL

Background. Ezekiel was among the exiles taken to Babylon in 597 B.C. He received his prophetic call in 593 B.C. and prophesied between 593 and 571 B.C., as the thirteen specific dates given in the book indicate.

■ *Ezekiel in a Nutshell: God explains to Ezek-*
■ *iel why Jerusalem will fall, then promises to*
■ *restore the people, the monarchy, and Jerus-*
■ *alem. Ezekiel warns his fellow exiles against*
■ *any wishful thoughts that Jerusalem might*
■ *be spared. As portrayed in Ezekiel's visions,*
■ *the glory of the Lord departs from the city,*
■ *leaving it vulnerable to destruction.*
■ *Although Judah would pay for its rebellion*
■ *against the Lord, God would eventually*
■ *restore His people to the land and reestablish*
■ *pure worship in a new Temple.*

Prominent themes of the book include God's presence, the sovereign authority of God over all nations (Israel as well as pagan nations), individual responsibility, righteousness, submission to God as the key to blessing, and hope for the future of the people of God

Ezekiel 1–3. God commissioned Ezekiel to go to a people who are "obstinate and stubborn" (2:4) and gave him a scroll to eat (3:1–3), symbolizing his complete identification with God's Word.

Ezekiel 4–24. Ezekiel's ministry began with the performance of a series of symbolic acts, all designed to communicate God's warnings of the coming siege of Jerusalem and the scattering of its people (4:1–5:17).

"For I take no pleasure in the death of anyone, declares the Sovereign LORD. Repent and live!" (Ezek. 18:32).

God brings punishment to unfaithful Israel with hope only in the distant future.

Ezekiel 25–32. God will also punish surrounding nations.

Ezekiel 33–48. God's glory will be seen in the restoration of a dead people and in restoration of pure worship in the new Temple.

DANIEL

Daniel and his friends were taken into exile in 605 B.C. They served mighty Nebuchadnezzar and his successors. Cyrus the Persian conquered Babylon in 539 B.C. Daniel retained a high civil office under the Persians.

■ *Daniel in a Nutshell: Daniel portrays God as*
■ *the sovereign Ruler of the universe, who con-*
■ *trols the destinies of both pagan empires and*
■ *His exiled people. He reveals His mighty*
■ *power to the kings of Babylon and Persia,*
■ *forcing them to acknowledge His supremacy.*
■ *He reveals to Daniel His future plans to*
■ *restore His people Israel once the times of the*
■ *Gentiles have run their course.*

The book of Daniel has traditionally been attributed to Daniel on the basis of explicit statements made within its pages (9:2; 10:2) and Christ's testimony (Matt. 24:15).

The book is divided into two major sections: chapters 1–6 are largely narratives; chapters 7–12 contain visions of future events.

Daniel 1–6. While in captivity, Daniel and his friends remain faithful to the true God. They face a number of situations that test their loyalty to God. Their faithful witness impresses even their captors.

Daniel 7–12. Chapter 7 begins a series of visions and revelations of future events. At the end, an angel instructs Daniel to seal up the revelation until the end times.

- *The Hebrew Bible from which our English*
- *versions are translated treats the Minor*
- *Prophets as a single book. Called The Book*
- *of the Twelve Prophets, the Hebrew book has*
- *the prophets in the same order that we use.*

- *Together the Minor Prophets work to*
- *present a single message reaffirming God's*
- *love and plans for Israel beyond His judg-*
- *ment on their sin.*

- *In terms of a time line, the Minor Prophets*
- *stretch from Hosea (a contemporary of Jer-*
- *oboam II, 786–746 B.C.) to Malachi (likely*
- *a contemporary of Ezra, 458 B.C.). The*
- *Minor Prophets do not follow a strict chro-*
- *nological order.*

- *The books of the twelve Minor Prophets,*
- *along with the other prophetic books, were*
- *written to help their readers or hearers*
- *believe their own times to be ones God had*
- *willed to be and brought to pass.*

HOSEA

- *Hosea in a Nutshell: God's love is constant*
- *and stubborn. It will not give up despite*
- *Israel's apostasy.*

Hosea 1–3. About 750 B.C. God showed Hosea
the depth of His love for His people by leading

Background. Hosea is the first book of the Minor Prophets (the Book of the Twelve). As such Hosea introduces the central question of the minor prophet—whether the Lord still loved Israel and had a purpose for them beyond His judgment on their sin.

Hosea's ministry to Israel (about 745 B.C.) roughly coincided with Amos's to Israel (about 750 B.C.) and preceded Micah's to Judah (before 722 B.C. to about 701 B.C.). *Hosea* means "He has delivered."

Hosea through the struggles of a marriage relationship with an unfaithful wife.

Hosea 4–10. These speeches by the Lord and His attendants (in Isa. 1:2 they are called "heavens" and "earth") rehearse the sins of Israel and the inevitable problems that follow.

Hosea 11–14. This section begins with another brief account of Israel's beginnings, stressing God's love for them (Hos. 11:1–4). Deuteronomy 32:10–21 is a parallel poetical description. There follows an announcement of a return to Egypt (a reversed exodus) and of a submission to Assyria as a result of their rebellion (v. 5). Chapter 14 calls on Israel to return to God, to recognize that Assyria could not solve their problems. It closes with a promise of God's continued openness to them.

JOEL

- *Joel in a Nutshell: Joel prophesies after a*
- *locust plague devastates the land. He warns*
- *Israel to repent, lest something worse happen*
- *to the nation.*

Joel's three chapters paint vivid pictures for the reader.

Joel 1. Chapter 1 pictures a terrible plague of locusts that signals God's devastating action against the land.

Joel 2. Chapter 2 repeats the announcement for Zion and describes the movement of troops, presumably the locusts, across the land (vv. 1–11). At this time repentance is still appropriate (vv. 12–17). There is hope beyond judgment on that day if the people repent (vv. 18–27).

Background. The name *Joel* means "Yahweh is God." The heading (1:1) does not set the prophet's message in a historical context. Containing only seventy verses, Joel is one of the shortest books in the Old Testament. The theme of the book is "the day of the LORD is near" (1:15).

"And it shall come to pass afterward, that I will pour out my spirit upon all flesh; and your sons and your daughters shall prophesy, your old men shall dream dreams, your young men shall see visions" (Joel 2:28, KJV).

Background. The name *Amos* means "sustained." Amos was not a professional prophet on the king's payroll (7:14). He was just "one of the shepherds of Tekoa," a village about twelve miles south of Jerusalem (1:1). But God's call compelled him to preach so boldly against the sins of King Jeroboam and the upper class of Samaria that Amos was accused of treason (7:7–8:2).

God can restore the land. Then the people will know God is present in Israel, that He alone is God (v. 27).

Joel 3. Chapter 3 pictures a phase of the great day of the Lord when nations are gathered for judgment.

AMOS

■ *Amos in a Nutshell: Amos shatters Israel's*
■ *peace and disturbs the people's pride. He*
■ *preaches mostly against Northern Israel's*
■ *pagan worship sites, yet he also declares*
■ *Judah's wickedness.*

Amos 1:1–3:12. This section emphasizes that all nations are subject to God and contains prophecies against Israel, Judah, and surrounding nations.

Amos 3:13–6:14. Israel and Judah have a form of religion that makes no difference in how the people conduct their business and treat the poor and oppress among them. God is just and holy. He will not tolerate continued hypocrisy.

Amos 7:1–9:15. Here we see five visions of judgment and mercy (7:1–3, 4–6, 7–9; 8:1–14; 9:1–15) that portray God's reluctance to turn Israel over to their executioners. Twice the sentence of judgment is turned back. But finally justice requires punishment, and God allows it.

The final verses of Amos predict a time when God will bring back Israel's exiles to live permanently in Palestine (9:13–15). This hope is repeated at the end of Obadiah but is given up before the end of the Minor Prophets.

OBADIAH

- *Obadiah in a Nutshell: Obadiah is a proph-*
- *ecy against Edom. When Jerusalem is*
- *destroyed, the Edomites delight in the disas-*
- *ter (v.12). They kill refugees from the city*
- *and take plunder (vv. 9–14). For their pride*
- *(vv. 2–4), hatred of brother and neighbor*
- *(vv. 9–10), and viciousness (vv. 15–18),*
- *Edom will be punished (vv. 5–8, 18).*

God is just and holds responsible those who take advantage of others in their times of distress.

Obadiah 1–17. Obadiah graphically portrays God's judgment on Edom (vv. 2–7). The reason for its doom was "the violence against your brother Jacob" (v. 10).

Obadiah 18–21. Obadiah presents the most complete plan for the resettlement of the Israelite tribes in Canaan to be found in any of the books of the prophets (vv. 19–20). The vision of Obadiah ends with a stirring call to faith in the worst of times: "And the kingdom will be the LORD's" (v. 21).

JONAH

- *Jonah in a Nutshell: Jonah is a prophet who*
- *is reluctant to obey the Lord and take a mes-*
- *sage of repentence to his enemies. The book*
- *shows the consequence of disobedience to*
- *God's call.*

Background. Obadiah is the shortest book in the Bible. The title verse calls this book "a vision." It portrays God's decisions about Edom, a small mountainous land east of the Dead Sea. Its people were considered descendants of Esau (Gen. 36). Judah and Edom lived in tension, sometimes in hostility, with each other throughout Israel's period in Canaan. Both claimed rights to the land south of the Dead Sea which changed hands repeatedly during that history.

Background. Jonah balances the book of Nahum with its message of God's wrath toward Nineveh. Nineveh was the capital of Assyria, the great empire that ruled over Palestine from the days of Tigiath-Pileser (about 750 B.C.) when the kingdoms of Jeroboam II and Uzziah were beginning to wane.

The book of Jonah portrays foreigners, the sailors, and the Ninevites as persons capable of responding to God and ones to whom God responds when they repent. In contrast to the stubborn and rebellious Israelites in Hosea and Amos, the Ninevites appear positively saintly.

Jonah 1. Jonah resists God's call and flees in the opposite direction. God works through the forces of nature—including a storm at sea and a large fish—to apprehend Jonah.

Jonah 2. Inside the fish Jonah prays and God delivers him.

Jonah 3. God orders Jonah a second time to go to Nineveh. This time Jonah obeys. His message is terse: "Forty more days and Nineveh will be overturned" (3:4). Despite the meager content of the message and no support for it, the Ninevites accepts God's warning and do works of repentance. Even the king repents. God takes note of their response, has compassion on them, and rescinds His order of destruction.

Jonah 4. Jonah observes the results of his preaching from a point outside the city. He is bitterly disappointed that God has not carried out His threat. God shows Jonah just how petty he is and how much his perspective is out of sync with God's.

MICAH

- ■ *Micah in a Nutshell: Micah is a contempo-*
- ■ *rary of Isaiah. He is both vigorous in his*
- ■ *denunciation of wrong and tender and per-*
- ■ *suasive in his appeals for repentance.*

We must ever be alert to adjust our attitudes toward people who seem to be hopelessly outside the mercy of God.

"To fear God is to stand in awe of Him; to be afraid of God is to run away from Him"—Carroll E. Simcox, quoted in Warren W. Wiersbe, *With the Word* (Nashville: Oliver Nelson, 1991), 591.

Background. The title verse calls this book "the word of the LORD," as those of Hosea, Joel, and Jonah have done. *Micah* means "who is like the Lord?" Moresheth was a town in Judah. Jotham, Ahaz, and Hezekiah ruled in Judah from 742 to 687 B.C. Between 740 and 700 B.C. the Assyrians invaded Palestine repeatedly.

The book of Micah is the centerpiece of the Minor Prophets (the Book of the Twelve). It contains within it the themes of the books that come before it and of those that follow it. It presents in capsule form the message of all twelve books.

Micah 1–2. In this section, Micah uses figures of harlotry to describe idol worship as Hosea had done (1:7). These speeches portray a devastating end for Samaria (1:6), but they also speak of danger at Jerusalem's gate (1:9, 12). Such danger came in the siege of 701 B.C. (2 Kings 18–19).

Micah 3. Like Amos, Micah condemns them for injustice and for profit-loving priests and prophets. They are too secure in an unjustified confidence (v. 11).

Micah 4–5. These two chapters present key views of God's plan or strategy (4:11) for Israel and Judah which look beyond the disasters. Micah 4:1–4 contains the beautiful picture (parallel to Isa. 2:1–4) of the restored Temple on Zion to which people from many nations would come to learn of God's ways and to hear His Word.

Micah 6–7. One more time the Lord voices a complaint against Israel. Micah mentions God's past actions on their behalf (6:1–5) and describes the fate of the dishonest, violent, and materialistic (6:9–16). This section contains one of the most succinct statements of what the Lord requires of His people (6:6–8).

"He has showed you, O man, what is good. And what does the LORD require of you? To act justly and to love mercy and to walk humbly with your God" (Mic. 6:8).

The Hebrew word *chesed* ("mercy," "lovingkindness") is difficult to render adequately in one word, but describes the all-encompassing, altruistic love of God from which every form of divine activity proceeds.

Background. The title verse (1:1) calls the book of Nahum both an oracle of doom and a vision. Both terms are appropriate. *Nahum* means "comfort" or "full of comfort." The prophet is unknown apart from this verse. The location of Elkosh is unknown. Although no date or period is provided, the subject of Nineveh's imminent destruction places it late in the 700s B.C. Assyria was a weakened power from 740 to 700 B.C.

NAHUM

■ *Nahum in a Nutshell: The Assyrian oppres-*
■ *sion created a troubling question. How could*
■ *God allow such inhumanity to go unan-*
■ *swered? Nahum responds that God will*
■ *judge and punish Assyria.*

The book of Nahum, like the book of Jonah, is completely concerned with Nineveh. Only two brief speeches concern Judah and Israel (1:15; 2:2).

Nahum 1. Nineveh has become God's enemy (1:2) and has earned His wrath (1:3). Now the day for judgment has come. Nahum 1:3b–10 is a poem about God's angry action against His enemies.

Nahum. 2. Nahum 2 is a vivid picture of the siege and capture of Nineveh.

Nahum. 3. Nahum 3 reaffirms God's intention to bring Nineveh to the ground.

HABAKKUK

■ *Habakkuk in a Nutshell: Habakkuk questions*
■ *God about world events. He wonders why the*
■ *evil people in his nation escape punishment.*
■ *The wicked are violent, unjust, destructive,*
■ *and divisive; yet God lets them live. Their*
■ *actions paralyze the courts and pervert jus-*
■ *tice. How long will such activities continue?*
■ *God responds by informing the prophet that*
■ *Babylon will punish Israel's wicked.*

Habakkuk's position in the Minor Prophets, after Nahum and before Zephaniah, is appropriate. It deals with the disappointment of Judeans and Israelites, dispersed in exile, that the fall of Nineveh had not brought immediate relief and restoration for Judah and Israel. Instead, an extended period of almost three decades was a time of greater repression and final disaster. Another half-century under Babylon would follow before Persia would succeed Babylon and bring new hope for Israel and Jerusalem. The book of Habakkuk deals with the frustrations of that period and teaches how one can maintain faith and hope in an extended period of adversity and trouble.

Background. Habakkuk is identified only as "the prophet." Haggai and Zechariah are similarly identified. The meaning of *Habakkuk* is not clear. It may be a foreign word. The book is called "an oracle," which may also be translated "a burden" as several other books, or sections of books, are called.

Habakkuk 1. Habakkuk is a perplexed prophet. The book begins with a cry to God: "How long?" This cry is found repeated in Scripture from Exodus 10:3 to many expressions in the Psalms.

Habakkuk. 2. This chapter shows that faith survives. The prophet takes a stand to wait for God's reply to his complaint (2:1). He does not have to wait long before he is commanded to write down his vision and publish it plainly because it still has to be fulfilled (vv. 2–3).

The most meaningful and important verse in Habakkuk follows (2:4). It describes the person who can survive such testing times. He who is puffed up will die. That is, those who are proud, arrogant, and filled with false pretenses cannot survive such testing. Then the good news: But the person in the right (relation to God and to his fellows) will *live* by simply being faithful.

Habakkuk 3. Chapter 3 is a psalm of confidence. It is Habakkuk's prayer psalm. The psalmist remembers reverently reports of God's great acts in the past and prays for Him to bring redemption in this time.

The closing verses announce his joy in the Lord despite the deprivations he has had to endure. God is his strength (vv. 17–19).

ZEPHANIAH

■ *Zephaniah in a Nutshell: Only three chapters*
■ *in length, the book of Zephaniah looks*
■ *toward the punishment of all sinful nations,*
■ *including Judah and the nations as well.*

Background. The title verse calls this book "the word of the LORD" as those of Hosea, Joel, Jonah, and Micah have done. *Zephaniah* means "Yahweh hides." *Cushi* means "the Ethiopian." Four generations of ancestors is unusual. The fourth name is Hezekiah, probably the king. The date for the book given in 1:1 is "the reign of Josiah . . . king of Judah" (640–609 B.C.). This was prior to the events cited in Nahum and Habakkuk. The theme of the book rather than chronology determines the position of the book within the Minor Prophets.

The theme of Zephaniah is the "day of the Lord." Joel pictured that day as it related to the Assyrian invasions that led to the destruction of Samaria and the Exile of Israel.

Zephaniah 1. The book opens with a prophecy of total destruction for the whole "land." A prophecy against Judah and Jerusalem follows. They are indicted for their idolatry (vv. 4–6).

Zephaniah. 2. Chapter 2 calls for an assembly of the humble and religious before the day of judgment arrives to seek the Lord and His will (vv. 1–3). Judgment against ethnic groups in Canaan follows: against the Philistine (Kerethite) cities of Gaza, Ashdod, Ekron, and Ashkelon (vv. 4–7); against Moab and Ammon (vv. 8–11); against Cush (Ethiopia) (v. 12); and against Assyria (vv. 13–15).

Zephaniah 3. Chapter 3 begins with a "woe," or curse, against Jerusalem for its lack of faith, its arrogant officials, prophets, and profane priests (vv. 1–5). The Lord cites His destruction of nations (v. 6) with the hope that Jerusalem might "accept correction" (v. 7). He calls for them to "wait" for Him to call (v. 8). The theme of "waiting on the Lord" dominates the book of Habakkuk.

Beyond the judgments lie God's goals (vv. 9–13). The peoples' lips will be purified so that all may worship the Lord and serve Him together, reversing the curse of Babel (Gen. 11:5–9).

A call to sing follows (vv. 14–17). Zion has every right to sing because the Lord God will be present in it again. He is their king. Verse 20 promises a homecoming and recognition among the nations that it is their God who is restoring them.

HAGGAI

■ *Haggai in a Nutshell: Guided by a religious*
■ *leader (Joshua), and a civic leader (Zerubba-*
■ *bel), many Jews return to Jerusalem between*
■ *538 and 535 B.C. What they find discourages*
■ *them. The city lies in ruins without protec-*
■ *tive walls. The Temple remains a heap of*
■ *rubble. Is this the glorious homecoming the*
■ *earlier prophets promised? How will God*
■ *restore Israel?*

Background. Haggai probably means "festive child," indicating that he was born on a holiday. Haggai has no genealogy.

The book of Haggai consists of five short addresses and a description of the results of Haggai's efforts to persuade his people to resume work on the Temple. The recipients of Haggai's message included Zerubbabel and Joshua, the high priest.

First Speech (Hag. 1:1–11). Haggai tells the people they are experiencing economic problems because they have not put first things first. He urges them to finish rebuilding the Temple.

Chronology of Haggai and Zechariah	
August 29, 520 B.C.	Haggai's first message (Hag. 1:1-11)
September 21, 520	Temple building resumed (Hag. 1:12-15)
October 17, 520	Haggai's second message (Hag. 2:1-9)
October–November, 520	Zechariah's ministry begun (Zech. 1:1-6)
December 18, 520	Haggai's third and fourth messages (Hag. 2:10-23)
February 15, 519	Zechariah's night visions (Zech. 1:7–6:8)
December 7, 518	Delegation from Bethel (Zech. 7)
March 12, 515	Temple completed (Ezra 6:15-18)

Second Speech (Hag. 1:12–15). In the second speech, Haggai assures the people of the Lord's presence and approval (v. 13), and the Lord stirs the spirit of both leaders and people as they work together (vv. 14–15).

Third Speech (Hag. 2:1–2). In the third address, given to both the leaders and the people, Haggai asks the older members of the community to recall the glory of the former Temple and thus to stir the new generation to new enthusiasm that will bring treasures from other nations to make the splendor of the new Temple even greater than the former one (2:6–9).

Fourth Speech (Hag. 2:10–19). The fourth address returns to the theme of the first address in linking worship, work, and the blessings of God.

Fifth Speech (Hag. 2:20–23). The final speech, delivered the same day as the previous one, is addressed only to Zerubbabel. It announces the imminent overthrow of the kingdoms of the world and the role that Zerubbabel, as symbol of Messiah, will play in the triumphant victory of God's kingdom on earth.

ZECHARIAH

■ *Zechariah in a Nutshell: Zechariah calls God's*
■ *people to attempt great things for God, specif-*
■ *ically rebuilding the Temple. He echoes the*
■ *message of earlier prophets, such as Amos and*
■ *Micah, that God does not value the ritual wor-*
■ *ship of those who deal unjustly with others.*

Background.
Zechariah's name means "Yahweh remembers."
Zechariah's message may be summarized under two headings: *prosperity* and *purification.*

Zechariah is a younger contemporary of Haggai. In the first eight chapters, he is concerned with the rebuilding of the Temple and with God's people being wholehearted in their worship of God. The second half of the book is concerned with God's future work through the Messiah.

Zechariah 1–8. These chapters present eight visions of a restored Jerusalem. Here is a call for repentance with a reminder that God has been very angry with their ancestors but is merciful and gracious to His people when they repent.

Zechariah 9–14. God will provide security for Jerusalem. He will restore the entire land, provide His people good leaders, and create a renewed, faithful nation. God will defeat Israel's enemies. Then all people, Jews and Gentiles alike, will worship the Lord together.

MALACHI

■ *Malachi in a Nutshell: The central thrust of*
■ *Malachi is that God revealed His love for His*
■ *people through their history. That revealed*
■ *love makes God's people accountable. They*
■ *are to obey the teaching of God's Law and the*
■ *preaching of the prophets.*

The book is a series of dialogues or conversations between the Lord and the people of Jerusalem.

Malachi 1. Malachi 1:1–5 begins this book with the same theme as Hosea: God's assertion of His unchanging love. The people who had suffered exile ask, "How have you loved us?" (v. 2). God replies, as the Minor Prophets have done so often, by citing a story from the Pentateuch. He speaks of His favoritism for Jacob over Esau (that is, for Israel over the nation Edom).

Malachi 2. Inattentive priests neither listen to God's instruction nor take care to honor God's name (2:1–7). They are to revere God and be in awe of His name. Instruction in God's ways is their main task. Their failure to follow God's way leads to their being despised and humiliated.

Malachi 3–4. God will send His messenger to His people. This event will be painful. It will be doom to some and salvation to others. It will result in a purified people who are also a joyful people.

REFERENCE SOURCES USED

The following list is a collection of the source works used for this volume. All are from Broadman & Holman's list of published reference resources. These works accommodate the reader's need for more specific information and for an expanded treatment of individual Old Testament books. All of these works will greatly aid in the reader's study, teaching, and presentation of the truths of the Old Testament. The accompanying annotations can be helpful in guiding the reader to the proper resources.

RESOURCES

Holman Bible Dictionary
An exhaustive, alphabetically arranged resource of Bible-related subjects. An excellent tool of definitions and other information on the people, places, things, and events.

Dockery, David S., et al. *Foundations for Biblical Interpretation* (Nashville: Broadman & Holman, 1994). This volume is a series of comprehensive essays edited and written by competent evangelical scholars and designed for contemporary readers. The essays cover historical background, cultural contexts, ancient languages, and doctrinal significance of the biblical text.

Holman Bible Handbook
A comprehensive treatment that offers outlines, commentary on key themes and sections, and full-color photos, illustrations, charts, and maps. Provides an accent on the broader theological teachings.

Holman Book of Biblical Charts, Maps, and Reconstructions
A colorful, visual collection of charts, maps, and reconstructions. These well-designed tools are invaluable to the study of the Bible.

House, Paul R. *Old Testament Survey* (Nashville: Broadman Press, 1992). A survey treatment geared to help beginning students understand the Old Testament.

The New American Commentary. Volumes available: Genesis 1–11; Deuteronomy; Joshua; Judges-Ruth; 1, 2 Samuel; 1, 2 Kings; 1, 2 Chronicles; Ezra-Nehemiah-Esther; Job; Proverbs-Ecclesiastes-Song of Songs; Jeriemiah-Lamentations; Ezekiel; Daniel; Hosea-Joel; Amos-Obadiah-Jonah; Micah-Nahum-Habakkuk-Zephaniah.

Shepherd's Notes, volumes Genesis–Malachi (Nashville: Broadman & Holman, 1997–98). These volumes provide a quick, easy access to the Bible—one book at a time. They deliver the essentials of each book in succinct, easy-to-digest bites.

MESSIANIC PROPHECIES OF THE OLD TESTAMENT

PROPHECY	OT REFERENCES	NT FULFILLMENT
Seed of the woman	Gen 3:15	Gal 4:4; Heb 2:14
Through Noah's sons	Gen 9:27	Luke 6:36
Seed of Abraham	Gen 12:3	Matt 1:1; Gal 3:8, 16
Seed of Isaac	Gen 17:19	Rom 9:7; Heb 11:18
Blessing to nations	Gen 18:18	Gal 3:8
Seed of Isaac	Gen 21:12	Rom 9:7; Heb 11:18
Blessing to Gentiles	Gen 22:18	Gal 3:8, 16; Heb 6:14
Blessing to Gentiles	Gen 26:4	Gal 3:8, 16; Heb 6:14
Blessing through Abraham	Gen 28:14	Gal 3:8, 16; Heb 6:14
Of the tribe of Judah	Gen 49:10	Rev 5:5
No bone broken	Exod 12:46	John 19:36
Blessing to firstborn son	Exod 13:2	Luke 2:23
No bone broken	Num 9:12	John 19:36
Serpent in wilderness	Num 21:8-9	John 3:14-15
A star out of Jacob	Num 24:17-19	Matt 2:2; Luke 1:33, 78; Rev 22:16
As a prophet	Deut 18:15, 18-19	John 6:14; 7:40; Acts 3:22-23
Cursed on the tree	Deut 21:23	Gal 3:13
The throne of David established forever	2 Sam 7:12-13, 16, 25-26; 1 Chr 17:11-14, 23-27; 2 Chr 21:7	Matt 19:28; 21:4; 25:31; Mark 12:37; Luke 1:32; John 7:4; Acts 2:30; 13:23 Rom 1:3; 2 Tim 2:8; Heb 1:5,8; 8:1; 12:2; Rev 22:1
A promised Redeemer	Job 19:25-27	John 5:28-29; Gal 4:4; Eph 1:7, 11, 14
Declared to be the Son of God	Ps 2:1-12	Matt 3:17; Mark 1:11; Acts 4:25-26; 13:33; Heb 1:5; 5:5; Rev 2:26-27; 19:15-16
His resurrection	Ps 16:8-10	Acts 2:27; 13:35; 26:23
Hands and feet pierced	Ps 22:1-31	Matt 27:31, 35-36
Mocked and insulted	Ps 22:7-8	Matt 27:39-43, 45-49
Soldiers cast lots for coat	Ps 22:18	Mark 15:20, 24-25, 34; Luke 19:24; 23:35; John 19:15-18, 23-24, 34; Acts 2:23-24
Accused by false witnesses	Ps 27:12	Matt 26:60-61

MESSIANIC PROPHECIES OF THE OLD TESTAMENT

PROPHECY	OT REFERENCES	NT FULFILLMENT
He commits His spirit	Ps 31:5	Luke 23:46
No broken bone	Ps 34:20	John 19:36
Accused by false witnesses	Ps 35:11	Matt 26:59-61; Mark 14:57-58
Hated without reason	Ps 35:19	John 15:24-25
Friends stand afar off	Ps 38:11	Matt 27:55; Mark 15:40; Luke 23:49
"I come to do Thy will"	Ps 40:6-8	Heb 10:5-9
Betrayed by a friend	Ps 41:9	Matt 26:14-16, 47, 50; Mark 14:17-21; Luke 22:19-23; John 13:18, 21-26
Known for righteousness	Ps 45:2, 6-7	Heb 1:8-9
His resurrection	Ps 49:15	Mark 16:6
Betrayed by a friend	Ps 55:12-14	John 13:18
His ascension	Ps 68:18	Eph 4:8
Hated without reason	Ps 69:4	John 15:25
Stung by reproaches	Ps 69:9	John 2:17; Rom 15:3
Given gall and vinegar	Ps 69:21	Matt 27:34, 48; Mark 15:23; Luke 23:36; John 19:29
Exalted by God	Ps 72:1-19	Matt 2:2; Phil 2:9-11; Heb 1:8
He speaks in parables	Ps 78:2	Matt 13:34-35
Seed of David exalted	Ps 89:3-4, 19, 27-29	Luke 1:32; Acts 2:30; 13:23; Rom 1:3; 2 Tim 2:8
Son of Man comes in glory	Ps 102:16	Luke 21:24,27; Rev 12:5-10
"Thou remainest"	Ps 102:24-27	Heb 1:10-12
Prays for His enemies	Ps 109:4	Luke 23:34
Another to succeed Judas	Ps 109:7-8	Acts 1:16-20
A priest like Melchizedek	Ps 110:1-7	Matt 22:41-45; 26:64; Mark 12:35-37; 16:19; Acts 7:56; Eph 1:20; Col 1:20; Heb 1:13; 2:8; 5:6; 6:20; 7:21; 8:1; 10:11-13; 12:2
The chief cornerstone	Ps 118:22-23	Matt 21:42; Mark 12:10-11; Luke 20:17; John 1:11; Acts 4:11; Eph 2:20; 1 Pet 2:4
The King comes in the name of the Lord	Ps 118:26	Matt 21:9; 23:39; Mark 11:9; Luke 13:35; 19:38; John 12:13
David's seed to reign	Ps 132:11 2 Sam 7:12-13, 16, 25-26, 29	Matt 1:1

MESSIANIC PROPHECIES OF THE OLD TESTAMENT

PROPHECY	OT REFERENCES	NT FULFILLMENT
Declared to be the Son of God	Prov 30:4	Matt 3:17; Mark 14:61-62; Luke 1:35; John 3:13; 9:35-38; 11:21; Rom 1:2-4; 10:6-9; 2 Pet 1:17
Repentance for the nations	Isa 2:2-4	Luke 24:47
Hearts are hardened	Isa 6:9-10	Matt 13:14-15; John 12:39-40; Acts 28:25-27
Born of a virgin	Isa 7:14	Matt 1:22-23
A rock of offense	Isa 8:14-15	Rom 9:33; 1 Pet 2:8
Light out of darkness	Isa 9:1-2	Matt 4:14-16; Luke 2:32
God with us	Isa 9:6-7	Matt 1:21, 23; Luke 1:32-33; John 8:58; 10:30; 14:19; 2 Cor 5:19; Col 2:9
Full of wisdom and power	Isa 11:1-10	Matt 3:16; John 3:34; Rom 15:12; Heb 1:9
Reigning in mercy	Isa 16:4-5	Luke 1:31-33
Peg in a sure place	Isa 22:21-25	Rev 3:7
Death swallowed up in victory	Isa 25:6-12	1 Cor 15:54
A stone in Zion	Isa 28:16	Rom 9:33; 1 Pet 2:6
The deaf hear, the blind see	Isa 29:18-19	Matt 5:3; 11:5; John 9:39
King of kings, Lord of lords	Isa 32:1-4	Rev 19:16; 20:6
Son of the Highest	Isa 33:22	Luke 1:32; 1 Tim 1:17; 6:15
Healing for the needy	Isa 35:4-10	Matt 9:30; 11:5; 12:22; 20:34; 21:14; Mark 7:30; John 5:9
Make ready the way of the Lord	Isa 40:3-5	Matt 3:3; Mark 1:3; Luke 3:4-5; John 1:23
The Shepherd dies for His sheep	Isa 40:10-11	John 10:11; Heb 13:20; 1 Pet 2:24-25
The meek Servant	Isa 42:1-16	Matt 12:17-21; Luke 2:32
A light to the Gentiles	Isa 49:6-12	Acts 13:47; 2 Cor 6:2
Scourged and spat upon	Isa 50:6	Matt 26:67; 27:26, 30; Mark 14:65; 15:15, 19; Luke 22:63-65; John 19:1
Rejected by His people	Isa 52:13-53:12	Matt 8:7; 27:1-2, 12-14, 38
Suffered vicariously	Isa 53:4-5	Mark 15:3-4, 27-28; Luke 23:1-25, 32-34
Silent when accused	Isa 53:7	Matt 27:14; Mark 14:61; Luke 23:9; John 19:9
Crucified with transgressors	Isa 53:12	John 12:37-38; Acts 8:28-35
Buried with the rich	Isa 53:9	Acts 10:43; 13:38-39; 1 Cor 15:3; Eph 1:7; 1 Pet 2:21-25; 1 John 1:7, 9

MESSIANIC PROPHECIES OF THE OLD TESTAMENT

PROPHECY	OT REFERENCES	NT FULFILLMENT
Calling of those not a people	Isa 55:4-5	John 18:37; Rom 9:25-26; Rev 1:5
Deliver out of Zion	Isa 59:16-20	Rom 11:26-27
Nations walk in the light	Isa 60:1-3	Luke 2:32
Anointed to preach liberty	Isa 61:1-3	Luke 4:17-19; Acts 10:38
Called by a new name	Isa 62:1-2	Luke 2:32; Rev 3:12
The King cometh	Isa 62:11	Matt 21:5
A vesture dipped in blood	Isa 63:1-3	Rev 19:13
Afflicted with the afflicted	Isa 63:8-9	Matt 25:34-40
The elect shall inherit	Isa 65:9	Rom 11:5, 7; Heb 7:14; Rev 5:5
New heavens and a new earth	Isa 65:17-25	2 Pet 3:13; Rev 21:1
The Lord our righteousness	Jer 23:5-6	John 2:19-21; Rom 1:3-4; Eph 2:20-21; 1 Pet 2:5
Born a King	Jer 30:9	John 18:37; Rev 1:5
Massacre of infants	Jer 31:1	Matt 2:17-18
Conceived by the Holy Spirit	Jer 31:22	Matt 1:20; Luke 1:35
A New Covenant	Jer 31:31-34	Matt 26:27-29; Mark 14:22-24; Luke 22:15-20; 1 Cor 11:25; Heb 8:8-12 10:15-17; 12:24; 13:20
A spiritual house	Jer 33:15-17	John 2:19-21; Eph 2:20-21; 1 Pet 2:5
A tree planted by God	Ezek 17:22-24	Matt 13:31-32
The humble exalted	Ezek 21:26-27	Luke 1:52
The good Shepherd	Ezek 34:23-24	John 10:11
Stone cut without hands	Dan 2:34-35	Acts 4:10-12
His kingdom triumphant	Dan 2:44-45	Luke 1:33; 1 Cor 15:24; Rev 11:15
An everlasting dominion	Dan 7:13-14	Matt 24:30; 25:31; 26:64; Mark 14:61-62; Acts 1:9-11; Rev 1:7
Kingdom for the saints	Dan 7:27	Luke 1:33; 1 Cor 15:24; Rev 11:15
Time of His birth	Dan 9:24-27	Matt 24:15-21; Luke 3:1
Israel restored	Hos 3:5	John 18:37; Rom 11:25-27
Flight into Egypt	Hos 11:1	Matt 2:15

MESSIANIC PROPHECIES OF THE OLD TESTAMENT

PROPHECY	OT REFERENCES	NT FULFILLMENT
Promise of the Spirit	Joel 2:28-32	Acts 2:17-21; Rom 10:13
The sun darkened	Amos 8:9	Matt 24:29; Acts 2:20; Rev 6:12
Restoration of tabernacle	Amos 9:11-12	Acts 15:16-18
Israel regathered	Mic 2:12-13	John 10:14, 26
The kingdom established	Mic 4:1-8	Luke 1:33
Born in Bethlehem	Mic 5:1-5	Matt 2:1; Luke 2:4, 10-11
Earth filled with knowledge of the glory of the Lord	Hab 2:14	Rom 11:26; Rev 21:23-26
The Lamb on the throne	Zech 2:10-13	Rev 5:13; 6:9; 21:24; 22:1-5
A holy priesthood	Zech 3:8	John 2:19-21; Eph 2:20-21; 1 Pet 2:5
A heavenly High Priest	Zech 6:12-13	Heb 4:4; 8:1-2
Triumphal entry	Zech 9:9-10	Matt 21:4-5; Mark 11:9-10; Luke 20:38; John 12:13-15
Sold for thirty pieces of silver	Zech 11:12-13	Matt 26:14-15
Money buys potter's field	Zech 11:12-13	Matt 27:9
Piercing of His body	Zech 12:10	John 19:34, 37
Shepherd smitten—sheep scattered	Zech 13:1, 6-7	Matt 26:31; John 16:32
Preceded by Forerunner	Mal 3:1	Matt 11:10; Mark 1:2; Luke 7:27
Our sins purged	Mal 3:3	Heb 1:3
The Light of the world	Mal 4:2-3	Luke 1:78; John 1:9; 12:46; 2 Pet 1:19; Rev 2:28; 19:11-16; 22:16
The coming of Elijah	Mal 4:5-6	Matt 11:14; 17:10-12